THE MISER

Molière

THE MISER

Freely adapted by
Sean Foley and Phil Porter

OBERON BOOKS
LONDON

WWW.OBERONBOOKS.COM

First published in 2017 by Oberon Books Ltd
521 Caledonian Road, London N7 9RH
Tel: +44 (0) 20 7607 3637 / Fax: +44 (0) 20 7607 3629
e-mail: info@oberonbooks.com
www.oberonbooks.com

PB ISBN: 9781786820273
E ISBN: 9781786820280

Cover design by AKA

eBook conversion by CPI Group (UK) Ltd, Croydon, CR0 4YY.

Molière and His Comedy

'Everyone knows that plays are written to be acted.' There are very few plays that Molière's own words can be applied to more aptly than his own... A practical man of the theatre – managing and producing his own company – and probably the greatest comic actor of his day in to the bargain, Molière wrote for performance rather than literary merit, and for laughter above everything else.

His plays, while undoubtedly masterpieces of comic drama that show a sophisticated taste for the depiction of human folly, selfishness and pretension, are crafted less along the lines of classical play-writing, and more from a battery of comic techniques that show a robust understanding of the tried and tested truths of laughter-making: farce, *Commedia dell'Arte*, cross-talk routines, misunderstandings, unlikely unmaskings, crazy reversals of fortune, puns, malapropisms, jargon, slang, visual comedy, physical roguery, provocatively vulgar gag-making, contemporary satire, and slapstick. Molière's genius was to combine this hard-won knowledge of comic stagecraft with careful dramatic choreography and ground-breaking comic characterization to produce plays that are both parables of human inter-reaction, and plain laugh-out-loud funny entertainments.

Thus *'The Misanthrope'* can be played as near tragedy, and as a farce of high society; *'Dom Juan'* is a medieval morality play, an opera buffa, and a comedy of manners; *'Le Bourgeois Gentilhomme'* an excoriating satire of pretension and at the same time a daft comedy-musical...

'L'Avare' – The Miser – is also a play that satisfies the two masks of theatre. It seemingly deals with a universal and timeless human predicament: the moral disasters that can befall us when an obsession with money obliterates all human compassion. Goethe, writing in 1825, pronounced it, 'deeply tragic' – and in many ways the dramatic situation, of an overbearing and dysfunctional father who threatens the happiness of his children and household because of his insane love affair with money, could indeed be the basis of a tragedy. But it isn't just the fact that the plot ends with young love triumphant, a broken family

re-united, and financial worries dispelled, that tells us that the play is comic as much as it is a study of obsession: it is the play's own structure and implied stage-craft. Pace and interest are maintained by Molière's brilliant and sophisticated mixing of types of style and scene: long next to short; 'psychological' next to slapstick; crazy visual humour next to plot; comic set piece next to soliloquy. How is Harpagon – The Miser himself – introduced to the audience? In a scene-setting 'grounded' set up? With a grand speech? As a rational character who we will see warped by his fatal flaw? No: he storms on, ranting, panting, whipping a servant and talking to the audience, in a display of physical comedy and verbal pyrotechnics straight out of the world of *Commedia dell'Arte*. It's as if Molière the comic has had a word with Molière the dramatic writer and said, 'let's be clear: get 'em laughing first, psychological insight later'.

So Molière developed his writing style both from his experience as a comic actor in the provinces engaged in the tricky business of trying to make people laugh, and from his great antecedents in theatrical comedy, the companies of the *Commedia dell'Arte* and the Roman and Greek comic playwrights of antiquity. From the latter he borrowed – just as Shakespeare did – plots and characters, (indeed *The Miser* is widely recognised as a re-worked version of *Aulularia* by the Roman writer Plautus). From the former he took characters recognisable to all: randy old men; posh youths; braggart captains; wily servants...

Indeed every single character in *The Miser* is a direct descendent of *Commedia's* stock characters. Harpagon is Pantalone – the avaricious and lecherous old tyrant who is especially mean to his children; Elise is Isabella – the prima donna of the *inamorati,* or 'lovers'. She is usually Pantalone's daughter. Cleante is Lelio – usually the son of Pantalone and follower of the latest fashion. 'The Lovers' in these plays were rich, self obsessed and selfish: primarily in love with themselves, secondarily in love with love, and only consequentially in love with the beloved. Maitre-Jacques is a more developed version of the famous Arlechinno servant character whose stupidity is relieved by intermittent flashes of shrewd wit: insolent, mocking, inept, faithful, clownish and brilliantly rude...

Again, Molière's genius was to take a previous form of comedy and bend it to his own ends. And just as his writing was informed by the *Commedia*, so undoubtedly was the performing style of his company – in fact he first gained the King's patronage by playing a farce 'in the Italian style'. It was from the travelling *Commedia* companies, and indeed Fiorelli's Italian company in Paris, that he learned the craft of stage business, gesture, mime and the *lazzi* – routines, signature gags, exaggerated physicality and classic repeated character traits used in the semi-improvised plays these companies put on. To these skills he added incredible team playing and an amazing new precision. La Grange, a contemporary, remarked that Molière's company played with practised art: 'Every actor knows how many steps to take, and their every glance is counted.'

So while his comedy developed and grew thematically, and became more and more about satirizing human nature and the society he saw around him, he always wedded these insights to the practical business of comic stage-craft. Thus, although Harpagon is one of Molière's greatest theatrical creations, a man riddled with contradictions, a self absorbed and tyrannical father – in fact, a convincing and totally realised character – part of his dramatic impact is that he is also a ludicrous figure, ridiculously dressed and crudely as well as physically funny.

Molière also famously said that, 'the duty of Comedy is to correct men while entertaining them'. And yet this never happens in his plays: Harpagon returns to his strongbox of money, a completely unreformed character. The comedies he wrote may show us the vanity, self-obsession, and gullibility of men and women, but he never offers any sort of way out of our pathetic and self-interested habits. Instead he just holds them up to us to laugh at. And even if we laugh at the meanest of his characters with a sliver of compassion it is probably because it is ourselves we are laughing at. The joy of Molière's comedy is that he never takes sides, never actually does take a 'corrective' line on human foibles. Rather than recommend any sort of better morality, he takes delight in a comic vision that jokes about, holds up to ridicule, and even revels in the paradoxes, tensions, and shortcomings of people just like us. Critics may feel dramatic art needs a moral purpose to be taken seriously, Molière certainly didn't… he was too busy making people laugh at such pretensions.

* * * *

In adapting *The Miser* for this production, Phil Porter and I wanted to create a modern comedy idiom that could be as rugged and playful for us today as that in which 17th century audiences must have experienced the original production. The play's structure and nearly all of Molière's lines are faithfully – if sometimes elastically – rendered. However we adjusted or re-imagined a few scenes where adding more modern references in place of the original jokes, or finding a less literal version of Molière's original would, we felt, render his original comic intentions more dynamically for today's audience. In particular, we abandoned the flowery and verbose prose style of the opening two lovers scenes – clearly these were written as a sort of satire on the language of courtly love, a satirical target that has basically disappeared for us. Secondly we amalgamated some of the very small servant parts into the one character of Maitre Jacques, thus expanding Molière's own original joke of having him play cook and coachman at the same time. To this end, we also transferred one of La Fleche's scenes to Maitre Jacques as well, and made him the house musician to boot: in our version he is thus now the original dogsbody – the put-upon, downtrodden, overworked servant whose work props up the Harpagon household.

Towards the end of his working life, Molière had a conception to combine music, comedy, drama, song, routines, jokes, dance and spectacle into an entirely new form that was a sort of total comic-dramatic entertainment. Anyone who works in theatrical comedy can still be inspired by that. His life-long pursuit of the laugh, and the idea that laughter itself could be a sort of purgative for life's ills – could sweep away our cares, and restore health and proportion – is with us still. And so *The Miser* – one of the great comic-dramas about human obsession – can still fulfill its primary role: as Molière himself put it, in 'L'amour Medicin':

Who'er should drive away
The cares of every day,
The sorrows, grief and pain,
The troubles that can kill,
Should shun the doctor's skill
And laugh with us again!

Sean Foley, February 2017

This adaptation was commissioned by Mark Goucher and presented by Mark Goucher, Mark Rubinstein and Gavin Kalin.

It was first performed on 8 February 2017 at The Theatre Royal Bath and transferred to The Garrick Theatre London where it opened on 1 March 2017.

CAST

HARPAGON	Griff Rhys Jones
MAITRE JACQUES	Lee Mack
VALÈRE	Mathew Horne
ELISE	Katy Wix
CLÉANTE	Ryan Gage
FROSINE	Andi Osho
LA FLÈCHE	Saikat Ahamed
MAITRE SIMON/MONSIEUR ANSELME	Michael Webber
DAME CLAUDE/PEDRO	Simon Holmes
MARIANE	Ellie White
ENSEMBLE	Sabrina Carter
ENSEMBLE	Ian Weichardt
ENSEMBLE	Cameron Robertson

CREATIVE TEAM

Director	Sean Foley
Set and Costume Designer	Alice Power
Lighting Designer	Paul Keogan
Music and Sound Design	Max and Ben Ringham
Casting Director	Sarah Bird CDG
Songs by	Chris Larner
Choreographer	Lizzi Gee
Musical Director	Phil Bateman
Assistant Director	Rosy Banham
Fight Director	Bret Yount
Company Voice Work	Barbara Houseman
Production Manager	Sam Paterson
Wardrobe Supervisor	Natasha Mackmurdie
Props Supervisor	Robin Morgan
Company Manager	Mark Shayle
Stage Manager	Titch Gosling
Deputy Stage Manager	Rebecca Maltby
Assistant Stage Manager	Sarah Coates
Head of Wardrobe	Loz Tait
Deputy Head of Wardrobe	Rebecca Barnett
Head of Wigs	Anthony Tester
General Management	Giles Rowland and Martina Thompson

ACT ONE

Paris, 1668. The large drawing room of HARPAGON's house: a grand but dilapidated residence. Morning light comes through the window illuminating the harpsichord.

MAITRE JACQUES enters and notices a rat on the floor. He takes off a shoe and chases the rat across the room, eventually catching it and bashing it to death with the shoe, then throws the rat into the audience.

MAITRE JACQUES begins lighting the candles. After lighting a couple he looks up at the task ahead – many more candles – and magically blows them all alight…

MAITRE JACQUES: *Et voilà!*

> *He heads for the harpsichord and starts playing a complex tune. He finishes, stands and takes a bow. While he is standing away from the harpsichord the music begins again. He quickly resumes his position at the harpsichord to maintain the pretence that he is playing the music.*

> *ELISE enters and collapses melodramatically onto a chaise longue, sighing heavily. (When she speaks she pronounces her 'r's as 'w's.) VALERE, the house butler and an ex-army officer, follows her in, visibly upset.*

VALERE: Elise, darling, what the devil's wrong? Our love for each other should … *(To MAITRE JACQUES.)* I say, do you mind?!

> *MAITRE JACQUES stops playing. The music continues. He thumps the harpsichord and the music stops.*

VALERE: Elise, darling, what the devil's wrong? Our love for each other should make you happy. It certainly used to! But now you've got a face like a spatchcocked poussin! You do still want to marry me?

ELISE: Of course, Valere. I love you more than ever! More than Cleopatra loved her Anthony when they first ravished one another. During that time when she would bathe each day in the milk from her ass. But I'm frightened, truly frightened!

VALERE: Of what, my love?

ELISE: Of you!

MAITRE JACQUES plays a dramatic chord.

VALERE: Maitre Jacques, shouldn't you be cleaning?

MAITRE JACQUES hides behind his newspaper.

ELISE: I'm terrified of losing your love. Your sex too often repays ardour with cruel inconstancy. Now that I have shared my most intimate bosom feelings with you, perhaps you will grow frosty and indifferent to me!

VALERE: Never, Elise! Do not judge me by other men. The intimate feeling of your bosom is all I live for. I shall love you for as long as I live. I should sooner befriend a Belgian than lose you.

ELISE: Oh Valere, you really do say the most romantic things. *(She holds his face to her bosom.)* You'd never leave me, would you?!

VALERE: *(Muffled.)* Never!

ELISE: You'll always love me, won't you?!

VALERE: *(Muffled.)* Always! My actions shall prove my heart's intentions! Do not torment me with unjust fears!

ELISE: Then I shall never doubt you again. And I shall prepare myself for a veritable barrage of criticism from society.

VALERE: You're not ashamed that I'm your father's butler?

ELISE: Perish the thought! You're not like all those other dirty, scrounging servants.

MAITRE JACQUES: Charmed, I'm sure.

ELISE: You're a well born gentleman, with a pedigree quite worthy of mine, if only others knew it! And knew of how you saved my life in that frightful shipwreck!

VALERE: That was nothing, my dear. Merely the instinctive reaction of a selfless individual with extensive military training.

ELISE: I replay it in my mind every night as I go to sleep. The ferocious wave that threw me overboard and pulled me

under. And how you dived in and rescued me, dragging my
shivering, slippery body through such rough waters! And how
you laid me out upon the sand, stripped me off and rubbed
and rubbed my freezing body until I was quite euphoric!

VALERE: I remember it well!

ELISE: And you've stayed by my side ever since, leaving the
army, hiding your true identity, your breeding, your rank,
and becoming my father's butler just to be near me. You
really are the most remarkable man. And if the *crème de la
crème* of society don't approve, well more fool you, I say,
more fool you! *(To a member of the audience.)* Especially you!
(Fails to convince herself.) Oh, it's really rotten being rich!

VALERE: Trust me, Elise, your father's lunatic behaviour
around money is quite enough to convince society that
you should be excused for marrying for love. Every soul
in Paris knows of his grasping cupidity, his penny-pinching
parsimony. His tight-fisted, mean-mannered, cheapskate
ways are legendary!

ELISE: Oh Valere, you're like a handsome thesaurus! But what
if his meanness extends to our marriage? If I don't marry
a chap he approves of I'll lose my inheritance! We simply
must secure his consent.

VALERE: And we shall, but let patience be our watchword.
One day I will find my parents, my fortune will be
restored, and then I daresay your father would marry me
himself! In fact, perhaps that's the solution.

ELISE: You marry Pa-pa?!

VALERE: No, silly, that I should leave and find my parents.

ELISE: No, Valere, please! It's more than my heart could bear!

VALERE: Very well, then I shall stay and win his approval
without money.

ELISE: But how, when he approves of nothing *but* money!

VALERE: You saw how I kissed his derriere to get on to his
staff. That's how! If you want to ingratiate yourself with
anyone you must use their words, adopt their philosophy,

applaud their choices, humour their prejudices. And they
will think you the cleverest person in Paris! Sincerity suffers
but flattery makes fools of even the wisest among us!

*MAITRE JACQUES punctuates with a couple of notes on the
harpsichord. VALERE slams the lid shut on his fingers.*

MAITRE JACQUES: *(Pained.) Foie gras!*

ELISE: Oh Valere, you're so brilliantly brainy! I say, perhaps
you could persuade my brother to assist in our *petite affaire.*
He too could sing your praises!

VALERE: With respect, Elise, I hardly think your father –

ELISE: Monsieur Harpagon.

VALERE: Yes, likely to listen to Cleante –

ELISE: My brother.

VALERE: That's him. He never has before. Never were a man
and his son less alike. They're spendthrift and pinchfist,
chalk and *fromage.* Besides, I can't be playing sycophant to
father and son, that's a battle on two fronts!

*ELISE starts to whine and slams the harpsichord shut on MAITRE
JACQUES' fingers.*

MAITRE JACQUES: *(Pained.)* Matt Le Blanc!

VALERE: But if you think it might help then of course we must
ask his support.

ELISE: Really?

CLEANTE, off, sings to himself like a soppy man in love…

VALERE: Absolutely. That's him now. You ask him, he'd do
anything for you…

ELISE: Jolly great idea!

VALERE: Thank you, darling –

*CLEANTE enters, trapping VALERE behind the door as he bounces
into the room. He wears elaborate, foppish, colourful attire and
speaks lispily.*

CLEANTE: Elise, darling sister, there you are! And thank heavens you're alone!

MAITRE JACQUES: What am I, chopped liver?

CLEANTE: There's something I simply must tell you!

ELISE: Cleante, darling brother, what's wrong? What happened to fray your nerves so freakishly?!

CLEANTE: So very much, Elise, that a million words could never do my story justice, and yet three little words say it all: I am in love!

ELISE: That's four words, Cleante.

CLEANTE: Quite so, four words: I am totally in love.

ELISE: And that's five words.

CLEANTE: Heart-pounding, tummy-fluttering, trouser-trembling love! The flowers smell more sweetly, the birds tweet more tweetily, why even the egg I had for breakfast tasted like it were laid by God himself!

ELISE: Have you proposed marriage yet?

CLEANTE: Not yet, but I shall soon.

ELISE: And do you think her likely to agree?

CLEANTE: Oh yes, I'm sure of it! Or as sure as I can be without having spoken with her.

ELISE: You haven't spoken? But Cleante!

CLEANTE: An irrelevance! Our love is a thing beyond such earthbound fripperies!

ELISE: But are they such fripperies, Cleante? Are they such fripperies?

CLEANTE: I don't expect you to understand how it feels to be in love! How could you until you've felt it for yourself? You know not of how it grips one like a most magnificent sickness!

ELISE: Well, actually, I do have some –

CLEANTE: I only wish you were infected too! Then you wouldn't tell me I'm a fool to love a girl I've not met!

ELISE: Actually, darling brother, I don't think it foolish. I actually think it tremendously romantic!

CLEANTE: Oh darling sister, I knew you'd understand!

ELISE: Now tell me all about her, every detail!

CLEANTE: Her name is Mariane and she's new to Paris. I passed a little courtyard where she was wringing out her mother's stockings and draping them on what I believe is called a 'washing line'. And oh, if e'er there were a goddess made to inspire love in all that saw her! Why, even Pa-pa could not fail to see the good in her! Her mother is in poor health, and so kind-hearted Mariane tends to the woman's every need. She is grace personified! Sincerity made flesh! And I suspect a real sizzler in the sack.

ELISE: You paint such a pretty picture!

CLEANTE: And yet where there is beauty there is tragedy, Elise. For Mariane is... Oh dear, I know not how to say it! Mariane is poor, Elise.

ELISE: Oh, how perfectly tragic!

CLEANTE: Indeed, a most wretched affliction! But fear not, for hers is not that whiffy, shirking sort of poor we see so much these days in the scrounging servant classes.

MAITRE JACQUES: Thank you.

CLEANTE: It's more the honest, striving kind that imbues its owner with a purity and integrity quite unattainable to us with money. And yet, how I long to deliver her from such privation by becoming her benefactor, and in so doing win her heart!

ELISE: Every true gentleman's fantasy!

CLEANTE: But how can I when Pa-pa won't give me a penny? I mean to say, is there anything so ghastly as this penny-pinching austerity? He's cut my allowance by thirty per cent in real terms in the last year. And there's another round of cuts announced for April. It's starting to affect my frontline services! My wig-maker, my parfumier! And if I don't pay my jeweller's bill soon, they'll take away my Universal Credit. I intend to confront Pa-pa!

ELISE: Gracious, darling brother, is that prudent?

CLEANTE: Prudence be damned, I will request, nay demand, an advance on my inheritance. And even if he denies me, I have started proceedings to borrow the necessary finance, and will elope with Mariane!

ELISE: Then I shall do the same, for I too plan to be wed… to Valere!

VALERE finally swings the door back open to reveal himself.

VALERE: Reporting for duty!

CLEANTE: Gumdrops, this is too exciting! We shall be slaves no more of his selfish avarice!

VALERE: I'll reconnoitre the enemy's position, and report back.

VALERE leaves with a flourish.

ELISE: Every day Pa-pa gives us more reason to mourn our dear mother's death. We must stand up for ourselves!

CLEANTE: I saw him at brekkers and he was *comme un chat qui a gagné la crème!*

ELISE: I have no idea what that means…

CLEANTE: We should profit from his good mood!

They run to the door of HARPAGON's study but it flies open, and LA FLECHE, a well-dressed servant, runs in. HARPAGON follows…

HARPAGON: Come back here, vile thief! I shall thrash your bloody arse to ribbons!

CLEANTE and ELISE are trapped behind the door and can't be seen.

LA FLECHE: But I ain't done nothing wrong, Mr Harpagon, sir!

HARPAGON: A liar as well as a thief! Well, you don't fool me! Bend over! *(He whacks LA FLECHE.)* Bandit! *(Ow! Ooh! Ah!)* Larcenist! *(Ow! Ooh! Ah!)*

LA FLECHE: *(Aside.)* He's evil! He's not human!

HARPAGON: Who are you talking to?

LA FLECHE: No one.

HARPAGON: *(Aside.)* He was talking to someone!

LA FLECHE: Who are *you* talking to?

HARPAGON: No one! *(Aside.)* Thinks he's a clever little bastard, doesn't he?

LA FLECHE: *(Aside.)* See what I mean, he wants everything to himself, even you lot!

Double take. HARPAGON resumes beating.

HARPAGON: I am terminating your employment for stealing! I am ripping up your *contrat de zero heures!* Now get out and stay out!

LA FLECHE: You can't sack me! I'm your son's valet, not yours! It's him what pays my wages!

HARPAGON: And I pay his allowance! And it looks as though he's spent half of it on your uniform! Mincing about my property, waiting for your chance to rob me blind!

LA FLECHE: Rob you? How?! You lock everything away and stand guard twenty-four hours a day! You dress like a pauper, but everyone knows you're minted. Loaded. Rolling in it. Flush. Walking down Easy Street and whistling a happy tune!

HARPAGON: I've never whistled a happy tune in my life! So it must be you who's spreading rumours I've got cash-money hidden about the house!

LA FLECHE: How should I know if you've got cash-money hidden about the house?

HARPAGON: Well, I haven't! No cash-money held on the premises overnight! So you can tell your burgling friends –

LA FLECHE: I haven't got time for this, I quit!

HARPAGON: You can't – I've just sacked you! *(LA FLECHE moves to exit.)* Wait! What have you stolen?

LA FLECHE: Nothing.

HARPAGON: Hands. Show me.

LA FLECHE: There.

HARPAGON: And the other ones.

LA FLECHE: What other ones?

HARPAGON: The other hands!

LA FLECHE: There!

HARPAGON: *(Points to breeches.)* And what's down there?

LA FLECHE: The crown jewels.

HARPAGON: I thought so! These modern breeches often receive stolen goods.

HARPAGON rummages in LA FLECHE's breeches.

LA FLECHE: *(Aside.)* I haven't nicked a thing off him but by god I'd love to!

HARPAGON pulls a feather from LA FLECHE's breeches.

HARPAGON: And here we have it – I knew you were up to something. You're stealing my soft furnishings one feather at a time! Now get out!

LA FLECHE: I hope one day your dreams will come true, Mr Harpagon, and someone does rob you…!

LA FLECHE opens the door to leave, revealing MAITRE JACQUES eavesdropping…

MAITRE JACQUES: I wasn't listening.

LA FLECHE: You chuffing cheese-parer!

Exit LA FLECHE.

HARPAGON: That's it, crawl away, larcenist, thief! You're not wanted here!

HARPAGON turns to the audience.

HARPAGON: And don't you lot look at me like that either. It's not easy being me. I have but one problem in life, yet it is a most grave one: I just have so much money! I tell you, these days we should pity the rich, not scorn them. These days if you want to go to the theatre you need to take out a second mortgage. *(To the 'cheap seats'.)* Even you cheapskates up there! The real difficulty for someone like me is where to put the stuff, how to keep it safe! You poor don't have to worry about that, you lucky sods! I could put it in a bank, but the rates of interest these days... I'd sooner trust a weasel with a dormouse than a banker with my money. This man agrees, he's nodding away. Oh, you are a banker! Yes, you look a bit of a banker. No, much better to do as I have done and hide one's money on one's own property! I've got a safe place buried in the wall behind that painting.

CLEANTE and ELISE slowly, quietly come out of their hiding place.

HARPAGON: But it's not in there, too obvious! No, I've hidden it outside in the greenhouse under the tomato plants...

He sees ELISE and CLEANTE.

HARPAGON: Oh God, they must have heard where I buried my money! I say, what are you doing here?

CLEANTE: Us, Pa-pa?

HARPAGON: Yes you, of course you, how long have you been standing there?

ELISE: Hardly any time at all, Pa-pa.

HARPAGON: But long enough, no doubt.

CLEANTE: For what, Pa-pa?

HARPAGON: To hear what I said!

ELISE: Said when?

HARPAGON: Just then!

CLEANTE: To whom?

HARPAGON: Myself!

ELISE: About what?

HARPAGON: About where I buried my money! Under the tomato plants in the greenhouse! Never mind. I was merely thinking aloud that money's so very hard to come by these days. And anyone, not me, but anyone who has, for instance, ten thousand crowns buried on their property is, hypothetically, a lucky man indeed.

CLEANTE: We didn't mean to interrupt, Pa-pa.

HARPAGON: Of course! I just didn't want you to get the ridiculous idea that I, for example, might have, for example, ten thousand crowns, for example, buried in the greenhouse…

CLEANTE: For example?

ELISE: In the greenhouse?

HARPAGON: For example! I don't have any money – ten thousand crowns – is that what you thought I said? If I did then life would be very different! Just think of all the luxuries I could buy with ten thousand crowns!

ELISE: But you don't believe in buying luxuries.

HARPAGON: No, because I'm poor.

ELISE: You're not poor, Daddy, you're really rather rich!

HARPAGON: Who told you that?! This is slander, vicious slander! It's exactly this kind of loose talk and loose living that'll see me murdered one day. Oh but you'd like that, wouldn't you? To see my throat slit, blood spraying everywhere, all over my soft furnishings.

CLEANTE: What loose living?

HARPAGON: What loose…?! Just look at you, look at you! What in God's name do you think you're wearing?!

CLEANTE: 'Tis the fashion.

HARPAGON: The fashion?! To go about the world like a badly erected fairground tent!

CLEANTE: I bought these clothes myself.

HARPAGON: How? You've no money of your own, only what I give you. And I don't give you any, do I?!

ELISE: He had a lucky streak at baccarat.

HARPAGON: Oh I see, a 'lucky stweak at baccawat!' And where did he get the money to play 'baccawat?' I saw no return on this investment. The very least you might do with these winnings is invest them wisely. But no, you spend it on fancy ribbons to hold up your breeches when everybody knows that a length of pig intestine will do just as well.

HARPAGON shows off his intestine braces.

CLEANTE and ELISE: Please Pa-pa!

HARPAGON: And wigs! Why spend money on wigs when there's hair growing out of your head for free? It's madness!

CLEANTE: But you wear a wig.

HARPAGON: Yes, but I made this myself when the neighbour's horse died. I didn't waste good money on it.

CLEANTE: I'm sure you're right, Father.

HARPAGON: Oh, I damn well know I am! You both rely too much on the bank of Mère and Père!

ELISE: But Mère's dead!

HARPAGON sits and gets out his purse, counting his pennies. CLEANTE and ELISE have a whispered argument over who will speak first.

HARPAGON: I say, what are you talking about? Are you plotting to steal my purse?

CLEANTE: We wish to discuss marriage, Pa-pa.

HARPAGON: Ah good, so do I. There's no need to look like that, I have your best interests at heart. Now, Cleante, are you aware of a girl who lives hereabouts called Mariane?

CLEANTE: I am.

HARPAGON: And you, Elise?

ELISE: Yes Pa-pa, and I'm told she is most meritorious in every respect.

HARPAGON: And you, Cleante, what do you think of her?

CLEANTE: I think her the most wonderful woman in all of Paris!

HARPAGON: So worthy of consideration, you'd say, marriage-wise?

CLEANTE: Oh, very much, sir, very much!

HARPAGON: She has a pleasant face? No unsightly warts or hairy bits?

CLEANTE: Her face is as perfect as dawn in summertime!

HARPAGON: And her manner?

CLEANTE: Captivating!

HARPAGON: I'm told she knows how to run a household.

CLEANTE: She is well-organised and most frugal!

HARPAGON: Frugal! Excellent! So she does know how to make a man happy!

CLEANTE: She will make her husband most blissfully happy, I just know it!

HARPAGON: Only snag is she's poor so the dowry won't be much.

CLEANTE: But father, a dowry's of no consequence when one is marrying the right person!

HARPAGON: I can't agree with you there. But since her sweet and abstemious manner is charming, and as long as she comes up with just a little money, I have resolved to overlook her poverty and…

CLEANTE: Yes, Pa-pa?

HARPAGON: I shall marry her.

CLEANTE: To me?

HARPAGON: No, to me.

CLEANTE: To you?!

HARPAGON: Yes, to me, to me! Why can't you listen when I'm speaking?!

CLEANTE: Excuse me, Pa-pa, I suddenly feel quite violently sick.

HARPAGON: Then go and have a glass of water!

CLEANTE: I had a soggy croissant for breakfast!

CLEANTE exits to get some water.

HARPAGON: From the tap, mind! And not too much, it's metered! This is the trouble with you young people, you're all weak, no fortitude! Anyway, Elise, that's what I've decided for myself.

CLEANTE returns with water.

HARPAGON: As for your brother, he will marry Mariane's aged mother –

CLEANTE spits out his mouthful of water in shock and disgust...

HARPAGON: ...a sweet old invalid woman –

CLEANTE: Oh God...

HARPAGON: ...by the name of Ann!

ELISE: But surely, given your respective ages, Pa-pa, shouldn't you marry Ann and Cleante marry Mariane?

HARPAGON: No, it's decided. I shall marry Mariane, Cleante will marry Ann.

ELISE: But marry, why don't you marry Ann and let Cleante marry Mariane?

HARPAGON: Marry, no! I will marry Mariane and he, marry, will marry Ann not Mariane, and marry, if he won't marry Ann he can't marry Mariane he'll have to marry Mary!

ELISE: Who's Mary?

HARPAGON: No idea. And you will marry our neighbour Monsieur Anselme.

ELISE: Monsieur Anselme? But I did not know the decrepit and rank-smelling old man by that name even had a son.

HARPAGON: He doesn't.

ELISE: But Daddy!

HARPAGON: Now now, don't make a fuss, it's a very good match. He's careful and wise and only just turned fifty some twenty years ago. And most important, he's very rich indeed!

ELISE: *(Curtsey.)* If you don't mind, Father, I will not marry Monsieur Anselme.

HARPAGON: *(Curtsey.)* If you don't mind, Daughter, oh yes you will.

ELISE: *(Curtsey.)* But if you'll pardon me, Father.

HARPAGON: *(Curtsey.)* If you'll pardon me, Daughter.

ELISE: *(Curtsey.)* I am your most humble servant.

HARPAGON: *(Curtsey.)* And I am your most humble servant.

ELISE: *(Curtsey.)* But if it pleases you, Father, no, I shall not marry Monsieur Anselme.

HARPAGON: *(Curtsey.)* Well, it does not please me, so yes you will marry him, this very evening! I have arranged a ceremony and a meal, at no little expense.

ELISE: No, Pa-pa, I can't go through with it, I shan't!

HARPAGON: You most certainly shall!

ELISE: You won't make me, you can't!

HARPAGON: I can and I will!

ELISE: I shall kill myself!

HARPAGON: As you wish, but marry him first!

ELISE: It's too dreadful, everything's dreadful…!

HARPAGON: It's no use flouncing about saying 'everything's dweadful'. The matter's decided. Everyone will approve, I'm sure.

ELISE: Only if they're out of their minds!

HARPAGON: Very well, let's ring for Valere and see what he thinks.

ELISE: Yes, Valere, we shall ask Valere!

HARPAGON: And you'll abide by what he says?

ELISE: If Valere approves, I shall agree to it!

They call for VALERE. Exit CLEANTE. VALERE enters unnoticed as they continue to call for him.

VALERE: You called, sir?

HARPAGON: Ah! Please adjudicate. Who is right, my daughter or me?

VALERE: Why, you are, of course, sir. *(He winks at ELISE.)*

ELISE: No, Valere, please do give proper consideration to the question.

VALERE: But there's no need, Elise. Your father is always right. *(He winks again.)*

HARPAGON: That's settled then. Elise will be married to our neighbour tonight!

VALERE: Ah, now, what? Right, golly…! *(Aside to ELISE.)* Sorry darling, grade A balls-up! *(To HARPAGON.)* Though you are always right, sir, perhaps it wouldn't hurt to hear Elise's argument.

HARPAGON: Nonsense. Monsieur Anselme is a highly desirable catch.

ELISE: If you like incontinent pensioners!

HARPAGON: He's not an incontinent pensioner, he's an incont… a widower of good birth, intelligence, and great health. He's outlived his first wife and their two children! And above all, he's rich!

VALERE: But perhaps Elise would appreciate a little more time to consider.

HARPAGON: What's to consider? This is a fantastic, unrepeatable offer! He's not even asked for a dowry! I'm getting rid of her free of charge!

VALERE: And I can see why that's tempting –

HARPAGON: Not a bean to pay!

VALERE: …but you wouldn't wish a loveless marriage on your daughter.

HARPAGON: I would if it's free of charge!

ELISE: But the difference in our ages!

HARPAGON: Yes, yes, but aren't you listening? He'll take her free of charge! Free of charge! Free of charge!

HARPAGON leads them in a giddy chant of 'free of charge', interrupted by the sound of a dog barking in the garden.

HARPAGON: Wait! I thought I heard the dog bark.

ELISE: He's barking because he's hungry, you never let us feed him.

HARPAGON: *(Aside.)* He's barking because someone's after my money! *(To ELISE.)* You're quite right, my dear, how remiss of me. I shall feed him now.

Exit HARPAGON.

ELISE: Really, Valere! What a risible performance!

VALERE: My love, I was playing for time.

ELISE: We haven't got time! Come ten o'clock I'll be in bed beneath Monsieur Anselme, that geriatric Romeo!

VALERE: All the more reason to act with military precision. We must draw his fire and then outflank him.

ELISE: No! I think we've had quite enough of your military claptrap, thank you! Think Valere! And quickly!

VALERE: What if I shoot you in the foot with a musket? Invalid you out?

ELISE: Oh, Valere, would you really shoot me in the foot for love?

They go into a clinch. HARPAGON returns.

VALERE: But it needn't come to that. If all else fails we shall simply elope… *(Sees HARPAGON.)* …elope… he lopes… he lopes a bit, yes, because he's old, Elise! But he's your father's choice, what does it matter how Monsieur Anselme walks?! Oh, Monsieur Harpagon, I didn't see you there!

HARPAGON: Valere, you speak a lot of sense. From now on, Elise, you must do everything he says. Instruct her, Valere.

VALERE: Er, right. You must never disobey me or your father again, Elise.

HARPAGON: Go on. Punish her!

VALERE: Nothing is more precious than money. You must get down on your knees…

ELISE kneels.

VALERE: ...and thank god you have a father who understands the world as it is. If a man can marry his daughter off free of charge there is no other consideration! Elise, you must marry Monsieur Anselme tonight!

HARPAGON: An oracle! A prophet! Delphi's got nothing on you, my boy! One day he'll make someone an excellent husband, won't he, Elise?

ELISE: Yes, Pa-pa.

ELISE runs off crying, VALERE and HARPAGON exit into his study.

ACT TWO

Enter MAITRE JACQUES now clothed in the servant's livery that LA FLECHE wore.

MAITRE JACQUES: Never feels right, squeezing into another man's uniform.

Enter CLEANTE from upstairs…

CLEANTE: Maitre Jacques! Maitre Jacques, why are you dressed as my valet?

MAITRE JACQUES: I am your valet. Since La Fleche got the sack, I've taken over his duties. *Plus ça bloody change!* I'm juggling five jobs as it is to make ends meet, though they never do, cos the jobs get paid as one, and in this low pay service economy –

CLEANTE: Stop rambling, Maitre Jacques, you're giving me a headache!

MAITRE JACQUES: 'Pologies, sir, I'm told you need a money lender.

CLEANTE: That's right! I need the money to finance a romance. And it's rather a desperate situation since my father intends to marry this same Mariane.

MAITRE JACQUES: Him, with her? You're pulling my *coq au vin!*

CLEANTE: Maitre Jacques, would that I were pulling your *coq au vin.*

MAITRE JACQUES: Love weren't invented for people who think like him, or look like him for that matter! He's like a scabby ferret. Why didn't you tell him you liked her yourself, sir, put him off?

CLEANTE: I thought it wise to secure the girl's affections first – before Pa-pa can lay his suit. In fact, I've just returned from her house where I made a splendid impression on both Mariane and her mother. So, did you find me a lender or not?

MAITRE JACQUES: Ay, sir. Though I must say 'tis a tawdry world is this moneylending. Poor people racking up debts to pay off other debts, borrowing more and more wonga to keep 'em afloat. 'Payday loans' they're calling 'em! Well, I'll tell you this: it's payday for the lenders, that's for sure!

CLEANTE: All right, that's quite enough social commentary.

MAITRE JACQUES: The agent's briefing the lender now, sir. You'll meet today at a neutral venue. If he's satisfied you're a good bet the deal goes ahead.

CLEANTE: So I'll get my fifteen thousand pounds?

MAITRE JACQUES: Ay sir, subject to status, terms and conditions apply.

CLEANTE: Bravo Maitre Jacques!

MAITRE JACQUES: You ain't heard the conditions yet. *(Reads from contract.)* 'In the interests of fairness, the lender proposes a rate of only five-and-a-half per cent.'

CLEANTE: Five-and-a-half, that's not bad!

MAITRE JACQUES: 'However, since the lender, in meeting the borrower's needs, must borrow at twenty per cent, the aforementioned borrower shall pay the aforementioned lender twenty per cent without prejudice to the five-and-a-half aforementioned.

CLEANTE: Twenty per cent PLUS five-and-a-half per cent! But that's…

MAITRE JACQUES: Twenty-five-and-a-half, sir.

CLEANTE: I knew that!

MAITRE JACQUES: Shall I say you're not willing?

CLEANTE: No, no, I shall need every penny if I'm to woo Mariane. He's got me over the proverbial barrel with my breeches around my ankles, taking it up the Arc de Triomphe!

MAITRE JACQUES: Just one further clause, sir. 'Of the fifteen thousand requested, the lender shall provide twelve thousand in cash. In respect of what remains the borrower shall accept the artefacts listed below.'

CLEANTE: You're not serious?

MAITRE JACQUES: 'One four poster bed with only three posts. One decorative wall-hanging depicting a pair of rutting stags. One set of durable bedsheets, moderately stained… And one popular board game by the name of 'Goosey-My-Goosey' with instruction booklet in Greek.'

CLEANTE: Anything else?!

MAITRE JACQUES: Yes, apparently your home is at risk if you do not keep up with payments.

A bell rings, off.

CLEANTE: I should like to goosey his goosey! I won't get 200 for the lot!

CLEANTE and MAITRE JACQUES move to one side to look at the contract. HARPAGON and MR SIMON enter. Deep in conversation, they don't notice CLEANTE and MAITRE JACQUES who, in turn, are too concerned with the contract to notice them.

HARPAGON: A desperate young bachelor in need of fifteen thousand, eh? Sounds like I could make a tidy sum.

MR SIMON: Indeed, sir. A desperate case this one. It seems he'll agree to any terms you care to name.

HARPAGON: How perfect…ly tragic. So, you're the broker and I'm the bank. Tell me, what kind of risk am I running?

MR SIMON: On that matter his servant was most reassuring. The young man comes from a wealthy family. The mother's dead and, if you insist, the young man will guarantee his father's death within eight months.

HARPAGON: Well, let's hope he dies sooner! Ha ha! No, shouldn't laugh. Our duty to our fellow creatures demands that we try to help in any way we can, especially if there's money in it.

MAITRE JACQUES and CLEANTE enter.

MAITRE JACQUES: Here, why's the broker talking to your father?

CLEANTE: Oh God, you didn't tell the broker who I was, did you? Pa-pa will kill me if he knows I'm borrowing so much – especially on these terms!

MR SIMON: You were very quick to get here.

MAITRE JACQUES: We ain't left yet.

CLEANTE hides under the harpsichord.

MR SIMON: And how did you know this was the meeting place? I hadn't given word. *(To HARPAGON.)* Believe me, sir, I never revealed your name and address. But perhaps, since we're here, we can get on with the transaction.

HARPAGON: Cleante, what are you doing here?

CLEANTE: Er, nothing, Pa-pa, just leaving.

HARPAGON: Good, I have business to attend to.

MR SIMON: But sir, this is the young man who wishes to borrow the money.

HARPAGON: You?! You are the half-witted wastrel that's agreed to pay these criminal rates of interest?!

CLEANTE: And you're the grasping scoundrel who imposes them!

HARPAGON: You'll bankrupt us all with loans like this!

CLEANTE: Well, you're morally bankrupt offering them!

HARPAGON: Spend, borrow, spend, borrow! I thought I'd put an end to boom and bust! You should be ashamed of yourself!

CLEANTE: Me ashamed?! And what about you, stooping so low as to become a money-lender?! *(To MR SIMON.)* No offence.

MR SIMON: None taken.

CLEANTE: Bringing shame on our family by lowering yourself to that vile and filthy trade! *(To MR SIMON.)* No offence.

MR SIMON: None taken.

CLEANTE: You're nothing but an unscrupulous shyster!

HARPAGON: And you are a preening popinjay with all the intelligence of a concussed gnat. Go away!

CLEANTE: With pleasure!

CLEANTE and HARPAGON toss their ripped up contracts in the air. CLEANTE starts to exit but returns. He attempts to adopt a manly posture by putting one foot on a chair but the seat of the chair gives way and he gets his foot stuck. He continues regardless...

CLEANTE: But I leave you with this, Pa-pa: Who is the greater sinner here? The young man who buys money because he must, or the man who bleeds others dry when he doesn't need a single penny!

Exit CLEANTE with chair. As he slams the door a picture drops off the wall.

HARPAGON: Get out. Out, both of you!

MR SIMON and MAITRE JACQUES exit.

HARPAGON: Oh, and Maitre Jacques!

MAITRE JACQUES returns.

MAITRE JACQUES: Sir?

HARPAGON: You're fired!

MAITRE JACQUES: Very good, sir. In what capacity?

HARPAGON: As Cleante's valet. He can live without one. As *my* valet you can clear this lot up.

MAITRE JACQUES slams the door. Some plaster falls down. He starts to pick up pieces of the ripped up contracts.

MAITRE JACQUES: Yes sir, and when will I actually get paid as your valet, sir, or indeed for any of my jobs? Only it's been a few months now and the beggar on the street corner is starting to give me loose change. I'm going to need some money, Sir.

HARPAGON: It's always the same with you class of people. Fixated on money! I wouldn't mind but you don't actually produce any! I'm the only wealth creator round here

and, as I've explained before, you'll get your fair share
eventually.

MAITRE JACQUES: How?

HARPAGON: Well, it'll trickle down to you! Yes, that's the
word: trickle! Now, time I checked on my, er, tomatoes
again.

*Exit HARPAGON through the French doors to the garden. As he closes
the door an animal's head falls off the wall onto MAITRE JACQUES.
Enter FROSINE, inadvertently slamming the door into MAITRE
JACQUES' head. FROSINE spots HARPAGON through the window.*

FROSINE: Howdy doo, Monsieur Harpagon.

HARPAGON: *(Off.)* Get lost, Frosine!

FROSINE: Someone's lost a livre and found a sou. Howdy doo,
Maitre Jacques, how's things?

MAITRE JACQUES: As ever, he hires, he fires, but I survive!
Despite just being savaged by a dead fox. What brings you
to these parts, Frosine?

FROSINE: Oh, you know me, bit o' this, bit o' the other. Fate
has given me an income. Good looks are money enough
to support some kinds of women. *(To audience member.)* She
knows what I mean…

MAITRE JACQUES: Got business with the gentleman of the
house, do you?

FROSINE: I do, though not in my normal line. I'm in career
transition. Less hands-on than I used to be. Introductions,
third party, fire and theft if you get my meaning. Reckon I
might make a nice tidy sum as it goes.

MAITRE JACQUES: And you might not. In the ranking o' misers
he's a top-level aristocrat this one. Higher than a baronet,
higher even than a duke.

FROSINE: You mean he's a Conte?

MAITRE JACQUES: I'm afraid so. A Conte of the first order.

FROSINE: Yeah well, there's certain services what always get
juicy rewards.

MAITRE JACQUES: Not from him. Squeeze him you'll only get pips. You've got more chance of being kicked up the arse by a snake than getting in that man's purse. More chance of getting sunburned at Christmas!

FROSINE: But I know men's weak spots, see?

She fondles him...

MAITRE JACQUES: I can see, yes, but I've got a big monologue coming up and this isn't helping! He has lust, what man don't? But only for money. He loves it more than reputation, honour or honesty. I see him sometimes talking to it, by candlelight, murmuring words of love to it, running his bony old fingers over it, even kissing the stuff and rubbing it up and down his breeches! I tell you, he'd marry his gold if he could.

FROSINE: Thank you for the information.

HARPAGON: *(Off.)* Oh, thank the Lord!

MAITRE JACQUES: Speak of the devil!

Enter HARPAGON.

HARPAGON: Relax, everyone, the, er, tomatoes are still unpicked! *(He sees FROSINE.)* Frosine, what are you still doing here?

MAITRE JACQUES starts to exit.

FROSINE: Thought I'd update you, Monsieur Harpagon, regarding Miss Mariane and her mother.

HARPAGON: Ah! Maitre Jacques?

MAITRE JACQUES: Yes, sir?

HARPAGON: Bugger off!

MAITRE JACQUES exits. As he shuts the door another picture tumbles from the wall.

HARPAGON: And?

FROSINE: All sorted! Like shooting *poisson* in a barrel, sir. I told you I'm good. I could marry a Turk to the Pope! I told the old girl Ann as how you'd took a shine to her girl Mariane after seeing her sat in the window doin' embroidery, sir.

HARPAGON: And what did she say?

FROSINE: Couldn't speak, sir, so overcome was she! Then when I stated your wish for Mariane to dine round here *ce soir* – to see your Elise get 'itched and give you a chance to pop the old question and do likewise – she gurgled like a beggar's guts and stuck Mariane's romantic future in my charge, sir!

HARPAGON: Excellent! Then since I am obliged to provide supper for Elise's wedding, I shall also marry this evening, killing two birds with one stone. We shall save on food *and* washing up!

FROSINE: Three birds, surely. Didn't you ask that I suggest to the old girl Ann that she might marry Cleante?

HARPAGON: And she agreed?

FROSINE: Oh yes! Seemed very taken with the notion of your lad having a rummage in her nuptial *trousseau*, she did.

HARPAGON: Three weddings for the price of a cheap evening meal! Oh happy day! And what can I expect from the dowry?

FROSINE: Think of it as a dowry in kind, sir. She's thrifty, see? Spent twenty thousand less last year than some girls I could name.

HARPAGON: No, no, you can't call money that *won't* be spent a dowry! We'd all be millionaires if we counted up the money we *didn't* spend. I need hard cash. Assets.

FROSINE: Oh, you'll get your hands on her assets, don't you worry.

HARPAGON: Frosine, there is one other thing that's been bothering me.

FROSINE: What's that?

HARPAGON: I'm imagining things from Mariane's point of view. She's young, beautiful. As a rule, youth turns to youth. I'm worried a man of my age may not rattle her teacups. And that might make for problems in the, er…

FROSINE: *Department de Pantelon?*

HARPAGON: *Oui.*

FROSINE: Well, that just shows how little you know her. She can't stand young attractive men. 'Stead she has a terrible weakness for the old ones with beards. Very grey beards. The older the man the better she likes it.

HARPAGON: Oh, really?

FROSINE: She looks at paintings of old men for erotic stimulation. Word to the wise: don't try and look any younger'n what you are. Her cut off is sixty – won't look at a man younger. *(Points out audience member.)* She'd love that old boy down there.

HARPAGON: The one with the walking frame?

FROSINE: That's him! He's turned his hearing aid up now! *(To HARPAGON.)* She was on the point of getting spliced only a few months ago, turned out the fella was *only fifty-six!* She broke it off. Last straw was when he read the marriage contract. He didn't even need glasses!

HARPAGON: How is she with false teeth?

FROSINE: They send her wild. See, Mariane's point of view, an older man is a real man, long as he ain't gone to seed. And look at you, you're in your prime. It's the skin. Beautiful skin. And the hair!

HARPAGON takes off his moth-eaten wig…

HARPAGON: You think me handsome?

FROSINE: Your face would tempt an artist! Stand up, let me see you walk.

HARPAGON struggles to his feet and hobbles across the room.

FROSINE: Uh, will you look at that?! Poetry in motion! And back! Uh! Style! Grace! A mature gazelle! You're pretty buff!

HARPAGON: I try to keep fit. Though I do occasionally cough up some phlegm.

FROSINE: She'll love that. She finds catarrh an aphrodisiac. And just look at those eyes, I could swim in those eyes! And the teeth are…

HARPAGON: *(Takes his teeth out.)* Take a closer look.

FROSINE: Lovely!

HARPAGON: And does Mariane know what to expect? Has she seen me stealing cat-like past her window?

FROSINE: No sir, but I've told her all about you and she's keen as *moutarde!*

HARPAGON: Well, that's marvellous! What can I give you, but my thanks. Thanks.

FROSINE: Now, Monsieur Harpagon, I've helped you, I'd like you to help me. The job's done, the match is made.

FROSINE holds out her hand and HARPAGON gives her a banknote on a piece of string.

HARPAGON: Oh all right, all right, here, take this!

FROSINE: *Merci buckets!*

As she moves to exit he pulls the string and the money returns to him.

FROSINE: Money on a string?! I weren't born yesterday. Come on, my more obvious assets don't command the fees they used to, though I can throw in something of that nature too if you fancy…

HARPAGON turns away…

FROSINE: People o' my class, we can't live on credit…and I got a court case pending. I need money, sir!

HARPAGON: All right! I'll see that my carriage takes you to the fair with the other ladies. And you can eat with us too, how's that?

FROSINE: No good, sir. I need cash, currency, not payment in kind!

HARPAGON: Then you now how I feel!

(Throws voice badly.)

Harpagon!

(To FROSINE.)

What was that?

(Throws voice badly.)

Harpagon!

(To FROSINE.)

Someone is calling me.

(Throws voice badly.)

Harpagon, Harpagon!

(To FROSINE.)

Must be one of the servants.

(Throws voice badly.)

Harpagon!

(Calls out.)

I'm coming!

(To FROSINE.)

We'll settle this all later.

Exit HARPAGON.

FROSINE: Mingy cheapskate!! May the very devil bite his balls off!

Enter MAITRE JACQUES.

MAITRE JACQUES: Told you. He always finds a way to disappear when he has to pay for services. The rich always do. Let me tell you a story.

MAITRE JACQUES plays his harpsichord. The OTHER SERVANTS join him and FROSINE, singing as they sweep up/change the scene/ set the table…

THE SERVANTS' SONG

MAITRE JACQUES:
I once had a job as a waiter
An eighteen hour-long day

SERVANTS A & B:
Me too!

SERVANT A:
The management were grateful

SERVANT B:
Fifty quid a plateful

SERVANTS A & B:
Earned me close on minimum pay

SERVANT A:
There was grouse, there was truffle'd potater

SERVANT B:
There was venison foam with chips

MAITRE JACQUES:
And then, for afters,

SERVANT A & B:
The boss would shaft us

MAITRE JACQUES:
Trousering all of the tips…

ALL:
You can polish up the silver, polish up the brass
Pile pretty platters at the kitchen pass
Pour champagne in a crystal glass
But the cash stays put with the upper class

The cash stays put with the upper class …
'Cos the rich are rich for a reason
And the reason's plain as sin
When the poor come knocking at the door
They pretend that there's no one…

MAITRE JACQUES:
Currently available…

ALL:
The poor are always amongst us
And skint till Judgement Day

And the reason's clear:
It's the rich, my dear,
Are giving none of it away

FROSINE:
I once had a life as a mattress
The oldest, coldest game
And the punters came and the punters went
The money was spent so they came again
There are men who call me a goddess
Or a bit of all right, or a bitch
It's water off a duck 'cos I don't give a –

ALL:
Oi!

FROSINE:
Well I do, but it didn't make me rich
You can do it in a palace, or an underpass
You can rent your parts
You can work your arse

ALL:
Polish up the silver, polish up the brass
Pile pretty platters at the kitchen pass
Pour champagne in a crystal glass

FROSINE:
But the cash stays put with the upper class

ALL:
But the cash stays put…
Because the rich are rich for a reason
And there's no damn room for doubt
When the poor come knocking at the door
They pretend that they've all gone…

MAITRE JACQUES:
Wintering in Monaco

ALL:
The poor are always amongst us
As the Bible likes to say
And the reason's plain:
It's the rich, again
Are giving none of it away

FROSINE:
> *One day we'll win the lott-ry*
> *A million pounds a day*
> *And we'll change the rules*

MAITRE JACQUES:
> *'Cos we're sentimental fools…*

ALL:
> *Not a chance*
> *We'll be in the south of France*
> *Giving none of it*

MAITRE JACQUES:
> *Not a bit of it?*

ALL:
> *Giving none of it away!*

FROSINE: Well, I'll get paid in the end, see if I don't. Either by him, or by the other parties. I'll make sure of it. A poor girl's got to live, right?!

ACT THREE

HARPAGON enters ringing a hand bell. ELISE, CLEANTE and VALERE arrive.

HARPAGON: All right, everyone, gather round. This evening is very important as we have at least two marriages planned. My own to Miss Mariane, Elise's to our neighbour Monsieur Anselme…

ELISE: *(With no enthusiasm.)* Hooray…

HARPAGON: And we're hopeful that Cleante may also plight his troth and marry Ann, mother of Mariane. *(CLEANTE recoils.)* And so it falls upon us to throw a party that is opulent, sumptuous and above all… inexpensive. Elise, you must ensure there's no waste. If any scraps go uneaten they must be bagged up and kept for the staff Christmas party. You will also accompany Mariane to the fair.

ELISE: Of course, Pa-pa.

HARPAGON: *(To CLEANTE.)* And as for you, my profligate progeny, we shall call a truce. If I'm to overlook your recent behaviour you must welcome Mariane into our family ways.

CLEANTE: Believe me, I have no greater desire than to get her in the family way!

HARPAGON: Good.

CLEANTE: If you need me I shall be titivating in my chamber.

CLEANTE exits flouncily.

HARPAGON: Now, where is Dame Claude?

DAME CLAUDE, an old retainer, steps forward with mop/broom.

DAME CLAUDE: Here, sir!

HARPAGON: You will also be in charge of decorating the house. I've brought down all the festive decorations from the loft. *(Hands over a tiny box.)* I'm sure there's quite enough there to make an impression.

DAME CLAUDE: Ooh! We haven't used these since your first marriage to dear Madame Beatrice all them years ago.

DAME CLAUDE starts to cry.

HARPAGON: Oh shut up, you old crone! Where's my sommelier?

MAITRE JACQUES: I'll fetch him, sir.

Exit MAITRE JACQUES.

HARPAGON: Please do, and quickly. We have quite enough to do without waiting for tardy servants.

MAITRE JACQUES returns as sommelier, complete with baggy breeches and a brocaded waistcoat.

MAITRE JACQUES: At your service, sir.

HARPAGON: What are you doing?

MAITRE JACQUES: I'm your sommelier – you sacked the old one.

HARPAGON: And what is that revolting stain upon your trousers?!

MAITRE JACQUES: I believe it's the trickle-down effect you mentioned earlier, sir.

HARPAGON: Well, cover it with your hat, you'll put the guests off their food.

MAITRE JACQUES: *(Covers stain.)* Very good, sir. But what should I do about the seat of my trousers? They're so far gone you can see right up my –

MAITRE JACQUES turns to reveal a gaping hole in his trousers.

HARPAGON: Oh, good heavens, turn back round! You shall just have to stand with your back to the wall and sally forth when the guests are seated. Now, show me how you pour the wine.

MAITRE JACQUES: Sir.

MAITRE JACQUES approaches the table and pours the wine, sticking his bare arse near ELISE's face as he does so.

ELISE: No no no no!

HARPAGON: No no no no, that's far too much! This is a fine wine, one doesn't guzzle it by the gallon! *(Snatches bottle.)* Our guests are not vulgarians intent upon insobriety!

HARPAGON unwittingly holds the bottle upside down, pouring the wine on the floor.

MAITRE JACQUES: Sir!

HARPAGON: They are upstanding members of society!

MAITRE JACQUES: The wine, sir!

HARPAGON: I'm talking about the wine!

ELISE: You're spilling it, Daddy!

HARPAGON: Oh God, why didn't you tell me?! Dame Claude, pass me that sponge.

DAME CLAUDE: I've got all me own teeth!

HARPAGON: Damn you, the sponge!

DAME CLAUDE hands over a mucky sponge.

HARPAGON: Funnel! We shall save most of it and top up the rest with water and vinegar...

HARPAGON manically mops up wine with the sponge, DAME CLAUDE produces a funnel, and he wrings it into the bottle. He tries a bit...

HARPAGON: It'll do. It will pass as a Hungarian Reisling. Where's my chef?

MAITRE JACQUES: Coming! *(Removes sommelier hat to reveal chef's hat.)* Er, that would also be me, sir.

HARPAGON: Chef, we're expected to provide dinner. Will that be a problem?

MAITRE JACQUES: Not if I have money for ingredients, sir.

HARPAGON: Oh, here we go again. Money! It's like an obsession with you people!

VALERE: Really, Maitre Jacques! Any fool can make a decent meal with money. The point in having a chef is that he can do it for next to nothing. *(Winks at ELISE.)*

MAITRE JACQUES: Fine! Since you're such an expert you can show me how to magic food from thin air!

HARPAGON: Oh, do be quiet, both of you. What will you need?

MAITRE JACQUES: How many guests?

HARPAGON: Ten, but imagine it's for eight.

VALERE: Very sensible, sir. *(Winks at ELISE.)*

MAITRE JACQUES: A meal for eight, let me see, that would be four tureens of soup…

HARPAGON: Four tureens? No, no, that's far too much.

MAITRE JACQUES: …plus six platters of vegetables

HARPAGON puts his hand over MAITRE JACQUES' mouth…

HARPAGON: Six platters?! That's enough to feed an army!

MAITRE JACQUES: Then you've got your trimmings –

HARPAGON: Trimmings?! Trimmings?! Trimmings?! Trimmings?! Trimmings?!

VALERE: Really, Maitre Jacques, we may as well feed them poison! For there's nothing worse for the health than too much food, ask any doctor. A lavish spread is no better than a death sentence.

HARPAGON: Quite so! Listen to the butler, he speaks the truth!

VALERE: To show your guests true kindness one must enforce frugality. And if they appear dissatisfied one must simply remind them of that wonderful saying: 'We must eat to live, not live to eat.'

HARPAGON: Let me embrace you, for that was quite the most moving thing I ever heard. 'We must live to eat, not eat to live!'

VALERE: Other way around, sir. 'We must eat to live, not live to eat.'

HARPAGON: 'Eat to eat, not live to live.' Very good!

VALERE: If it pleases you, sir, I shall oversee the preparation of dinner.

HARPAGON: Thank you, Valere. We shall offer a simple, nourishing menu of inexpensive, off-putting food. Mutton stew bulked out with lots of fat and roadkill, followed by a seasonal fruit pie. Nip through into neighbour Anselme's garden, take a few windfall apples, he won't mind. And shake a few chestnuts down while you're at it.

VALERE: Very good, sir.

HARPAGON: *(To MAITRE JACQUES.)* And while he's doing that, you clean my carriage!

MAITRE JACQUES: One moment, sir, I believe you're addressing the coachman.

MAITRE JACQUES swaps his chef's hat for a coachman's hat.

MAITRE JACQUES: Say again, sir.

HARPAGON: My carriage, damn you, clean it! And get my horses ready to go to the fair!

MAITRE JACQUES: Your horses can hardly stand, sir.

HARPAGON: Don't be absurd, I haven't used them in weeks.

MAITRE JACQUES: Because they do nothing, must they be fed nothing? Better to work hard and get a square meal, I say. I love them horses. I'd go without myself to see them fed. But they've not had a meal in weeks.

HARPAGON: Then starve yourself and feed them. There must be some left-overs in the kitchen.

MAITRE JACQUES: *(Switches hats.)* No sir, there's no left-overs 'cept a couple of mouldy old spuds.

HARPAGON: Then give them those.

MAITRE JACQUES: *(Switches hats.)* Can't do that, sir. Potato's poison to a horse, makes 'em sick.

HARPAGON: Well, something else!

MAITRE JACQUES: *(Switches hats.)* There is nothing else. Pantry's empty but for cabbage leaves.

HARPAGON: Well, that'll do for today!

MAITRE JACQUES: *(Switches hats.)* Can't do that, sir. Cabbage gives a horse wind. Can't have it blowing off in your bride's face, sir.

HARPAGON: This is ridiculous!

VALERE: I shall borrow Anselme's horses from next door.

MAITRE JACQUES: *(Throws hat down.)* There'll be nothing left of next door at this rate.

VALERE: If you don't mind me saying, sir, your sommelier, cook and coachman speaks too much.

MAITRE JACQUES: *(Putting chef hat on.)* And if you don't mind me saying, your butler's a backsliding bootlicker!

HARPAGON: Oh, stop it, the both of you! You're like a pair of children!

MAITRE JACQUES: I'm sorry, sir, but I can't abide a kiss-arse, and this one's the worst I ever met. He's butterin' you up's what he's doing! With his 'yes sir' and his 'very good, sir'! Making me look bad when I'm as loyal a worker as you'll ever have. I have a soft spot for you, sir, spite of myself. Least, as the cook I have. *(Switches hats.)* As the coachman you drive me up the wall, sir. *(Switches hats.)* And as for the sommelier, I can't stomach you. sir. *(Takes hat off.)* And as for the harpsichordist, he thinks you're an absolute –

MAITRE JACQUES censors himself with a trill on the harpsichord

But you ask anyone, it's me, the chef, what stands up for you when people say bad things!

HARPAGON: Oh, and what do people say?

MAITRE JACQUES: I'd tell you but I fear you'd fire me from one or more of my jobs.

HARPAGON: *Au contraire*, apart from money there's nothing I value more than honesty.

MAITRE JACQUES: Very well, sir. Truth is, there's no more popular sport in Paris than telling tales of your meanness.

HARPAGON: Such as?

MAITRE JACQUES: Well, sir, I don't believe any of it, but they do say as how you keep a padlock on your purse and have deliberately lost the key. Then there's one doing the rounds of how you took a mouse to court for nibblin' a bit of Camembert. Then that you re-plastered your house using porridge, which is true, and that's what accounts for that bit of dried up jam up there in the architrave. And that your servants have to make their uniforms using anything to hand…

He pulls a curtain and we see a waistcoat shape has been cut from it. He stands in front of it, his waistcoat blending in with the curtain.

MAITRE JACQUES: Truth is sir, you're a joke.

HARPAGON: You cheeky upstart!

(Slaps MAITRE JACQUES as chef.)

Fetch the coachman.

(MAITRE JACQUES changes hats.)

How dare you speak to me like that?!

(Slaps MAITRE JACQUES as coachman.)

And the sommelier please.

MAITRE JACQUES: He's on his tea break.

HARPAGON: The sommelier!

(MAITRE JACQUES changes hats.)

Scum!

(Knees MAITRE JACQUES as sommelier in the groin.)

And finally my harpsichordist. Play!

MAITRE JACQUES: I don't want to.

HARPAGON: Please, entertain my guests.

MAITRE JACQUES starts to play.

HARPAGON: Never forget you owe me for the curtains!

HARPAGON slams shut the harpsichord on MAITRE JACQUES' hands.

MAITRE JACQUES: Patti Boulaye!

Some more plaster falls from the ceiling.

HARPAGON: Now will all of you idling scrimshankers please just get to work! Elise, follow me!

Exit HARPAGON, DAME CLAUDE and ELISE, leaving only VALERE and MAITRE JACQUES.

VALERE: Ha! Never mind, Maitre Jacques! One always gets a poor return for honesty, it's the way of the world!

MAITRE JACQUES: Think you're really someone, don't you?! Coming in here, Mr Would-Be-Gentleman. Reckon you're a real Don Juan In Soho! Join our household and two minutes later you think you run the place. Well, you'll get your comeuppance!

VALERE: Maitre Jacques, honestly, I meant no harm.

MAITRE JACQUES: Laughing? At me? Think I'm funny, do you? Make you laugh? Funny how? Like a clown? Maybe I'll give you something to laugh about!

VALERE: Go easy!

MAITRE JACQUES: Easy? Easy? What if I don't like this whole 'easy' thing?!

VALERE: All right, steady on.

MAITRE JACQUES: 'Steady on' is it now? I'll teach you a lesson you'll never forget!

VALERE takes a sword from a display on the wall.

VALERE: Very well, Maitre Jacques, you have impugned my honour. En garde!

MAITRE JACQUES: *(Grabs a baguette.)* Roulade!

VALERE: Well, Maitre Jacques. What sort of lesson did you have in mind? Coulé!

MAITRE JACQUES: Lesson, who mentioned a lesson? Soufflé!

VALERE: You're all talk, I could take you apart! Riposte!

MAITRE JACQUES: Granted, yes, I can see that now. French Toast!

VALERE: You're nothing but a second-rate coachman, a third-rate cook and a fifth-rate harpsichordist! Parry! Lunge!

MAITRE JACQUES: I never meant to upset you. Vanilla! Sponge!

VALERE: You don't know me! Remise!

MAITRE JACQUES: Oh, please!

VALERE: Raddoppio!

MAITRE JACQUES: Stoppio!

VALERE: Prepare!

MAITRE JACQUES: Éclair!

VALERE slashes at the baguette, chopping it down inch by inch until only a stub is left.

MAITRE JACQUES: Thank God it wasn't a brioche!

VALERE shoves the baguette end in MAITRE JACQUES' mouth.

VALERE: Stay away from me, Maitre Jacques. It'll be better for you.

MAITRE JACQUES: Petit Filous!

VALERE exits.

MAITRE JACQUES: I don't mind getting beaten up by my employer, that's normal, but not his butler! Seems I can't afford to be honest no more. The poor never can – social comment! Well, I shall get my own back on that two-faced so-and-so if it's the last thing I do in this freely adapted joyously satirical comedy of manners!

Enter FROSINE.

FROSINE: Howdy doo, Maitre Jacques. Is his nibs at home?

MAITRE JACQUES: Ay, somewhere.

FROSINE: Only I've decided to go through with this business and either he, or the other party, will pay. A poor girl's gotta live, right? Be a love and fetch him. Tell him Miss Frosine has returned with his bride-to-be Miss Mariane. Chop chop!

MAITRE JACQUES exits, showing his bare buttocks as he goes as an act of defiance.

MAITRE JACQUES: Kiss it!

MARIANE enters.

FROSINE: Mariane!

MARIANE: Golly, Frosine, look at me! I'm shaking like a leaf! I feel as if I were awaiting execution.

FROSINE: Ha! Death by Monsieur Harpagon! And I bet you'd rather be sharing a *petit mort* with that mysterious young gentleman visitor o' yours. *(MARIANE squirms dreamily.) Yes*, I can see you would!

MARIANE: He's just so sweet and attentive, and so dishy, and he has this charming lisp!

FROSINE: But you still don't know his name?

MARIANE: It's true. But what are names anyway but words we use so we know who we're talking about? I'd marry him right now if I could, and for love, Frosine, love!

FROSINE: Let's not be too hasty, eh? There's another way to play this. Young men are nice to look at, sure, but they're paupers 'til they inherit. Stick to the programme: marry some old boy with loads of dosh and sit tight. Might be a bit grim in the old conjugal department –

MARIANE: Seem rather cynical, betting one's happiness on the hope one's husband pegs it. And what if Monsieur Harpagon carries on living?

FROSINE: I've thought of that. You only agree to marry if he agrees to leave you a widow soon as poss. If he don't croak in three months he triggers a get-out clause and the deal's off. Anyway, he ain't *that* bad looking!

Door flies open. Enter HARPAGON with greyed wig, beard, spectacles, ear trumpet, walking frame, etc.

HARPAGON: My darling!

MARIANE: Oh god! *(She faints.)*

HARPAGON: Sorry I'm late, I was polishing my dentures. Forgive me wearing these glasses – I can't see a thing without them! *(To FROSINE.)* I say, what's wrong with her? Isn't she pleased to see me?

FROSINE: Course she is! She's just a bit shy, that's all! *(Revives MARIANE.)* Miss Mariane!

MARIANE: Sorry, Frosine. I don't know what... *(She sees HARPAGON again.)* Jesus Christ! *(She faints again.)*

HARPAGON: Perhaps my daughter can calm her nerves. Elise, come and meet Mariane!

ELISE bounds in. MARIANE revives.

ELISE: Ah yes. Miss Mariane, I'm delighted to make your acquaintance. I am Monsieur Harpagon's daughter.

MARIANE: Daughter?! She's older than me!

HARPAGON: And big with it! Not many of those to the pound! You must meet my son as well! Cleante!

Enter CLEANTE in theatrically tragic fashion.

CLEANTE: Mariane.

MARIANE: *(To FROSINE.)* Heavens, no, it can't be...! That's him, Frosine! My lisping visitor, my love!

FROSINE: *(Aside.)* Shut the portcullis!

HARPAGON: You seem shocked to see my children are so grown up. But never mind, at least you won't have to wash their bottoms, ha, ha!

CLEANTE: Miss Mariane, I am overjoyed to see you. Yet our reason for being here leaves me nothing short of incredulous! That I should be expected to call one so exquisite my stepmother – well, forgive me if that word does not catch in my throat like a lump of unmasticated biscuit!

HARPAGON: Forgive Cleante. He does not wish us to marry so tries to dissuade you with such unschooled flattery.

MARIANE: Rest assured, Cleante, I feel quite the same. You are, to me, too much a man to bear the name 'stepson'. Only know that I never sought this situation, nor would I willingly consent to that which would cause you pain.

HARPAGON: *(To CLEANTE.)* See, she's not doing it to hurt you! *(To MARIANE.)* Is your mother here yet, Mariane? I know Cleante is most keen to pay his compliments.

MARIANE: No, sir. She hoped to come but was detained by an unmentionable illness.

HARPAGON: *(Sees CLEANTE bashing his head in frustration.)* Forgive him, my dear, he'll be reconciled to our wedding plans soon enough.

CLEANTE: I should sooner be torn apart by wolves than hide my real feelings!

HARPAGON: Why must young people always go on about their feelings? Nobody cares!

CLEANTE: Very well. If my feelings are so irrelevant I shall put myself in your position and speak your feelings as I imagine them. And I shall tell Miss Mariane that the prospect of our nuptials provokes such euphoria in me as to reduce all other joys to nil. For to be her husband would be the greatest glory this world could offer! And as such there is no obstacle I would not sweep aside, no foe I would not rend asunder –

HARPAGON: All right, that's enough, I have a tongue in my head! I shall whisper my own sweet nothings later on in the marriage bed.

MARIANE retches.

FROSINE: *(To MARIANE.)* Game face! Game face!

HARPAGON: Now fetch the chairs for dinner!

ELISE rings the servant bell. The bell rope comes away in her hand. VALERE enters with two chairs.

VALERE: Chairs, Sir.

FROSINE: Might I suggest, sir, that we go to the fair first? Then the victuals is going to be ready on our return.

HARPAGON: All right, then tell the coachman to harness the horses! Mariane, you'll understand my not having any refreshment to offer just yet –

CLEANTE: *Au contraire,* Pa-pa! Refreshment is available since I took the liberty of ordering some exotic fruits in your name.

HARPAGON: Exotic fruits?!

CLEANTE: Just a few mandarin oranges from South Siam, a box of sweet lemons from Sicily, oh, and a barrel of juicy kumquats from Dutch Ceylon!

HARPAGON: Juicy kumquats?!

CLEANTE: The man offered a discount since you were buying so much but I insisted on paying full price!

HARPAGON: Valere, did you know about this?

VALERE: I did not, sir.

CLEANTE: And since you are so unselfish, Pa-pa, I know you would like Mariane to have that diamond ring upon your finger, by way of a love token.

HARPAGON: My ring?!

MARIANE: Oh no, I couldn't!

CLEANTE: But come, is it not magnificent?

MARIANE: Of course, it's beautiful –

CLEANTE: Do you hear, Pa-pa? She thinks it beautiful. Here, let me help you take it off…

CLEANTE grabs HARPAGON's finger, they fight…

HARPAGON: What?! No! Get off me!

CLEANTE: Heavens, it's a tight old bastard and no mistake!

MARIANE: Really, it's not necessary!

HARPAGON: Blithering halfwit!

CLEANTE: See how he curses it for staying on his finger!

HARPAGON: Valere, get him off me!

VALERE gets involved. A melee-cum-tug-o-war ensues...

MARIANE: Please, stop, I don't want it!

CLEANTE: But you must or you'll insult him!

HARPAGON: Bloody hell and damnation!

CLEANTE: See how upset he is already!

VALERE: *(To audience member.)* Here, grab my hand.

HARPAGON: *(Falling back as VALERE falls into audience.)* Arrrrghhhhhhh!

CLEANTE: The ring! Please accept this as a token of love.

MARIANE: No, I couldn't.

HARPAGON: You bloody idiot!

CLEANTE: You're making him furious – take the ring or else!

HARPAGON: I should have you whipped!

CLEANTE: Don't blame me, Pa-pa! I'm trying to persuade her but she's stubborn!

FROSINE: I should take the ring if I were you, dear, 'fore someone gets hurt!

CLEANTE: Take it!

MARIANE: No.

CLEANTE: Take it!

MARIANE: No.

ALL: Just take the poxy ring!

MARIANE: All right, I shall take the ring!

Enter MAITRE JACQUES in elaborate footman costume.

HARPAGON: Oh god, who are you now?

MAITRE JACQUES: Footman, sir.

HARPAGON: Well, what do you want?

MAITRE JACQUES: Coachman wants to see you, sir.

HARPAGON: Then go and fetch him!

MAITRE JACQUES: Very good sir.

HARPAGON: He'd better have those horses ready.

Exit MAITRE JACQUES, who immediately reappears as the coachman. As he opens the door it slams into HARPAGON, sending him sprawling.

HARPAGON: Aaargghhhhhh!

HARPAGON falls back into the fireplace burning his bum, then staggers back against the door causing a mounted boar's head to fall onto him. He collapses.

ELISE: Pa-pa, are you hurt?

HARPAGON: Yes!

ALL: *(Aside.)* Good!

HARPAGON: I know what this is. You're all after my money! You're trying to kill me. Perhaps I'm dead already.

VALERE: Unlikely, sir, but I'll look into it.

MAITRE JACQUES: You're not dead, sir, but I'm afraid the horses are.

ALL: Ahhh.

ELISE: Daddy, I told you they'd starve!

MAITRE JACQUES: One died of hunger, sir, the other of grief when he heard the news.

HARPAGON: How unutterably tragic. When you see the chef tell him to put them in the stew.

MATIRE JACQUES: Very good, Sir.

HARPAGON: We shall have to borrow Anselme's.

VALERE: Well, I did suggest that.

CLEANTE: In the meantime, perhaps I might step into your shoes again, Pa-pa, and show Miss Mariane the garden!

MARIANE: I should like that very much.

CLEANTE: Valere, bring out several bottles of father's best champagne!

CLEANTE, MARIANE, FROSINE and ELISE go to the garden.

HARPAGON: Valere? There's some cheap Italian fizz in the larder, give them that instead. *(Aside.)* Don't say you've never done it!

VALERE: Very good, sir.

Exit VALERE. Only HARPAGON and MAITRE JACQUES remain.

HARPAGON: Alone at last.

MAITRE JACQUES: Don't mind me.

HARPAGON: What a son! What a daughter! What a cook-coachman-footman-sommelier-harpsichordist!

A 'plink' from MAITRE JACQUES at the harpsichord. Dramatic music builds.

HARPAGON: Why did he want to go out to the garden? He's figured out why I keep tending the tomatoes that's why! I must work fast. I must get married, get my hands on Mariane's assets, marry Cleante to the girl's mother, marry Elise to Anselme, secure a dowry and re-bury my money in a safer place! And I must do it *tonight!*

INTERVAL

ACT FOUR

In the Garden. CLEANTE, MARIANE, ELISE and VALERE stand around a garden swing-chair, all a bit tipsy on fizz. FROSINE and MAITRE JACQUES are also in attendance. They sing…

THE LOVERS' SONG

LOVERS:
We're in love!

FROSINE:
That's nice!
Isn't it nice?
Isn't it nice, Maitre Jacques?
Isn't it lovely?

MAITRE JACQUES:
What?

FROSINE:
This!

MAITRE JACQUES:
What?

FROSINE:
This!

LOVERS:
We're in love!

MAITRE JACQUES:
Yeah.
Ladies and gentlemen, we
Reckon, 'cos the interval
Was getting on for twenty minutes long…

LOVERS:
We're in love!

MAITRE JACQUES:
There are elements of the plot
That you might well have forgot
So we thought we'd recapitulate in song

LOVERS:
We're in love!

ELSIE AND MARIANE:
But it's a tragedy!

VALERE AND CLEANTE:
Oh woe is we for we're in

LOVERS:
Misery!

MAITRE JACQUES:
Job done

FROSINE:
Shush!
Tell your auntie Frosine all about it, why don't ya?

CLEANTE AND MARIANE:
He's in love with her
And reciprocally, she's in love with him

VALERE AND ELISE:
We're in love!

CLEANTE AND MARIANE:
But the situation's 'orrible and grim

CLEANTE:
Poor babe, her
Fiancée is seventy-three

ALL LOVERS:
The next-door neighbour

MARIANE:
A wrinkly Romeo: so woe is she

ELISE:
Oh, woe is me

CLEANTE, MARIANE AND VALERE:
Oh, woe is she

ELISE:
Oh woe is me

FROSINE:
Oh, deary me!

MAITRE JACQUES:
Yeah, what a bummer
What a terrible dilumma!

FROSINE:
Shush!

VALERE AND ELISE:
He loves Mariane but he
Cannot marry her, he's feeling glum

CLEANTE:
I'm glum!

VALERE AND ELISE:
His bride-to-be is Anne
Who's Mariana's mum!

MARIANE:
My mum!

CLEANTE:
I'd rather
Die than follow such a plan

But father
Has in mind to marry Mariane

VALERE, MARIANE, AND ELISE:
The father marries Mariane

FROSINE:
He plans to marry Mariane?

CLEANTE:
So I can't marry Mariane

LOVERS:
Instead he's (I've) got to marry Anne!

MAITRE JACQUES:
Clear?

LOVERS:
Thus Cupid proves himself unjust
And love, in whom we placed our trust
Is broke, betray'd, beguil'd and bust
In dark and dank dismay!

MAITRE JACQUES:
God help us!

LOVERS:
Death – that oft-maligned thief
Would frankly, now, be warm relief

FROSINE:
> *But Frosine's here to save the day...*

ALL:
> *Really?*

MAITRE JACQUES:
> *Really?*

FROSINE:
> *Yeah!*

ALL:
> *Oh!*

FROSINE:
> *God knows how*
> *But worry not your brow*
> *For love will find a way*

LOVERS:
> *That's encouraging!*

FROSINE:
> *I've seen worse*
> *And you are not the first*
> *Frosine and lovers*
> *Love will save the day!*

VALERE: Dear friends, I fear I have made things worse with my attempts to win over Monsieur Harpagon with sycophancy. Hoist upon my own petard! But I shan't be running the white flag of surrender up the flagpole just yet. Maitre Jacques, fall in and follow me!

MAITRE JACQUES pulls a face but follows VALERE off as ordered.

FROSINE: Cor, I wish you lot had told me what was really going on! Seems like this romantic palaver's got seriously out of hand – and I could have had it sorted!

CLEANTE: I think not, Frosine. 'Tis destiny! My horoscope's bust! The stars are aligned against one. Blasted kismet! Oh, Mariane, what shall we do?

MARIANE: Hope against hope, I suppose, and pray for good fortune!

CLEANTE: Surely one cannot simply resign oneself to the whim of circumstance!

MARIANE: I don't know what else to say. I've never made a decision in my life. You think for me, Cleante. Instruct me. I shall do absolutely anything within the bounds of etiquette.

CLEANTE: Etiquette?! Hang etiquette! Civilization never advanced by observing sodding etiquette!

MARIANE: But Cleante, I am a lady-girl! Even if I were to abandon all social decorum, I could never go against my mother.

ELISE: Frosine, our streetwise lower-class friend, any ideas?

FROSINE: Just one: we turn his 'ead. Make old pinchpenny lose interest in Mariane. Then the whole shebang collapses.

CLEANTE: But how could anyone lose interest in my sensational sweetheart?

FROSINE: Well, we offer an alternative, don't we? We find a very talented woman of around thirty…five, me for example, and get her to act the part of a rich widow! A posse of servants, a beautiful dress, a fancy title. The Marquise of Montpelier, the Viscomtesse of Vichy. She's impetuous, a little crazy maybe. She falls madly in love with your father on first sight – *un grand amour fou!* So much so that she's prepared to sign all her estates over to him, and place her considerable assets in his hands. And what does your father love more than love?

ALL: Money!

MARIANE: You really think he'd fall for such a trick?

FROSINE: I'd bet my last pair o' clean knickers on it. Then he'll release Mariane from her mother's promise. By the time he finds out he's bought dodgy goods, you'll be off on your honeymoon.

ELISE: He won't be able to resist!

CLEANTE: I'm not sure I understand, but it sounds such serious *fun!*

MARIANE: And I shall play her lady-in-waiting. I'm quite the *ingénue* with Chateau-Neuf Players. *(To CLEANTE.)* Just wait until you see my Clytemnestra!

CLEANTE: I can't wait for opening night!

ELISE: I'll prepare the ground! Tell Pa-pa there's a rich widow in town! Gosh, if you really pull this off, Frosine, we seriously owe you.

CLEANTE: *(Still bemused.)* Yeah, like, as they say in the back streets of Montmartre, 'big time'! Mariane, you can do your bit too. You need not go against your mother's wishes, but persuade her to abandon the original marriage offer. And above all put her off me. If possible! Use everything you've got. Your beautiful smile, your sparkling eyes, your simply dimply cheeks…!

MARIANE: My darling!

They kiss. Enter HARPAGON.

HARPAGON: Lovely tomatoes…! *(He sees them kissing.)* What the blazes…? I thought he didn't like her! He's got his hand in my biscuit barrel.

ELISE: Oh look, Cleante! It's Pa-pa come to see us!

CLEANTE: Mmn-mmn?

ELISE: Pa-pa, it's Pa-pa, say hello to Pa-pa! It's PA-PA!! PA-PA!! HELLO PA-PA!!!

CLEANTE: Oh, hello, Pa-pa…!

HARPAGON: No, no, carry on, I should hate to interrupt.

FROSINE: Don't worry, Monsieur Harpagon. Ain't nothing to interrupt. Your boy was just looking up close in Miss Mariane's eye, ain't that right? For a piece of grit what was giving her jip.

MARIANE: Yes, bad case of gritty-eye. Thank you, Cleante!

CLEANTE: *Pas de problème.*

HARPAGON: Well, that's a relief. *(Aside.)* These youths take me for a dunderhead. The fuckwits! *(To the ladies.)* I only came with the news, ladies, that your carriage to the fair awaits, no expense spared, literally, we borrowed Anselme's horses.

ELISE: Oh, thank you, Pa-pa! And I, in turn, have most exciting news for you, of a titled and wealthy widow, newly arrived in –

HARPAGON: Thank you, Elise, but not now. I shan't join you all. These old knees of mine would not wish it. Maitre-Jacques will drop you and circle. I hear the council is charging a hefty fee for parking a carriage in a residential area.

CLEANTE: Perhaps, Pa-pa, if you are not yourself going, I should accompany these ladies to the fair. *In loco parentis*, so to speak!

HARPAGON: *(Aside.)* I know his game. He wants another nibble on my chicken! *(To CLEANTE.)* No, Cleante, sit. I am sure these ladies can fend for themselves. I shall need your help here preparing the banquet. *(Aside.)* I shall keep him where I can see him, and grill this traitorous weasel! *(End of aside.)* Now toddle off, ladies, have your fun!

The ladies go to the fair. CLEANTE does his best to seem innocent of anything and everything.

FROSINE: *(Aside, to CLEANTE.)* Don't tell him the plan!

CLEANTE: *(Aside.)* I can thoroughly assure you I won't. I still don't understand it!

FROSINE exits to the fair.

HARPAGON: *(Calling after them.)* And remember, the fun of the fair is simply the fun of the fair. There's no need to waste money on the amusements! So then, loyal son. Now the ladies are gone let us talk man to man.

CLEANTE: Should we not prepare the banquet first?

HARPAGON: Plenty of time for that. First a question. Putting aside that she'll soon be your stepmother, what do you think of Mariane? Her manner, her wit, her countenance, do you think her attractive?

CLEANTE: Well, she's all right, I suppose. If you like that sort of thing.

HARPAGON: Come, come, she'll soon be my wife. Does she seem pleasant to you?

CLEANTE: To me? Her? No. God, no! After all, that is to say, I mean, golly what?! No! In truth I find her as charmless as she is hideous! And as for her wit, well, if I have nothing to say of it this is because I see no evidence of it!

HARPAGON: So what was all that earlier? About her dazzling looks and unmasticated biscuits?

CLEANTE: Oh that! I was only making her feel welcome, as you requested.

HARPAGON: Oh well, that quashes my little brain wave. I saw her just now with you youngsters and fancied others might think me foolish marrying one so young.

CLEANTE: No!

HARPAGON: I had it in mind to pass her to you.

CLEANTE falls back on the greenhouse in shock, breaking a pane of glass.

CLEANTE: P-pardon, Pa-pa, p-pass her to me, you say?

HARPAGON: Silly idea!

CLEANTE: Well, let us not be hasty! For though she's not… entirely to my taste, I could yet marry her, as a favour to you.

HARPAGON: I shall not force my son into a match he doesn't desire.

CLEANTE: Oh but I do, Pa-pa! That is, if it pleases you…

HARPAGON: Marriage is a matter of love and nothing else, you taught me that. You've made it quite clear you think her a repugnant, slack-witted cretin.

CLEANTE: Oh, but I don't, Father, I don't!

HARPAGON: Cleante?

CLEANTE: I can no longer persevere with this preposterous pretension! *(The bench breaks as CLEANTE slams his foot through it.)* I have been in love with Mariane since first I saw her, yesterday morning. I was about to ask your permission to marry her when you announced your own cross-generational intentions.

HARPAGON: But my dear boy, this changes everything. And she has feelings for you, does she?

CLEANTE: In abundance, sir! Our feelings accord as harmoniously as a pungent piece of pickle 'pon a piquant piece of parmesan. She adores me as I adore her.

HARPAGON: And so slam shut the jaws of my weasel trap!

CLEANTE: Pa-pa?

HARPAGON: Thought you'd filch your father's goods, did you? Gritty eye my pockmarked buttocks! Well, think again, perfidious offspring! She's booked in my name! You'll marry the woman who brought her into the world and that's the closest you'll get!

CLEANTE: Urr! Why, you duplicitous brute! Well, there's no man stronger than one fortified by love! You won't take her from me without a fight!

HARPAGON: Very well! Maitre Jacques!

MAITRE JACQUES: *(Pops up at window.)* I wasn't listening!

HARPAGON: Bring my duelling pistols!

MAITRE JACQUES: Sir!

HARPAGON: We shall settle this madness once and for all.

CLEANTE: A duel, Pa-pa?

HARPAGON: Indeed. You wanted a fight. Let's have one to the death.

Enter MAITRE JACQUES with pistol box.

MAITRE JACQUES: Your duelling pistols, sir.

CLEANTE: You mean to kill me?

HARPAGON: I certainly do.

HARPAGON takes a large and impressive pistol.

HARPAGON: Take your weapon.

CLEANTE takes the small, pathetic pistol that remains.

CLEANTE: Doesn't seem very fair.

HARPAGON: All's fair in love and war. We shall turn and shoot after five paces. Are you ready?

CLEANTE: But surely?

HARPAGON: Are you ready, I said?!

CLEANTE: Yes, Pa-pa.

They stand back to back and begin to walk.

HARPAGON: One, two, three, four, five!

HARPAGON turns and shoots – just missing MAITRE JACQUES – and shoots CLEANTE's wig off.

CLEANTE: Bastard!

CLEANTE shoots HARPAGON's wig off.

HARPAGON: Reload!

MAITRE JACQUES: Hold it! If I might intervene, sir. P'raps we might settle this *petite dispute famille* without pistols. Then no one has to die.

CLEANTE: Yes, I think that's an excellent idea!

MAITRE JACQUES: Plus we'll save on having to re-glaze the greenhouse, sir.

HARPAGON: Well, I suppose there's some sense in that. Maitre Jacques, will you adjudicate?

MAITRE JACQUES: Might as well, I do everything else round here.

HARPAGON: Thank you.

HARPAGON fires a shot in MAITRE JACQUES' direction, knocking his hat off.

MAITRE JACQUES: *(Showing his hat on a string.)* See, I even had to do that!

HARPAGON: Sorry, didn't think it was loaded.

HARPAGON fires a shot above. A pigeon cries out and falls through the sky to the floor.

HARPAGON: There's a bit of luck. We shall have that for supper.

MAITRE JACQUES: *(Picks up pigeon.)* So, Monsieur Cleante, if you'd be so good as to stand over there. *(Sotto, to CLEANTE.)* I'll sort this for you for a small consideration.

MAITRE JACQUES takes CLEANTE to the other side of the stage, comes back to HARPAGON.

MAITRE JACQUES: Monsieur Harpagon, please explain the nature of your grievance, sir!

HARPAGON: I am in love with a girl. Cleante is in love with a girl.

MAITRE JACQUES: Same girl?

HARPAGON: How did you guess?

MAITRE JACQUES: And he plans to defy you and marry her himself?

HARPAGON: He plans to defy me and marry her himself.

MAITRE JACQUES: Well, he's in the wrong there for sure, sir!

HARPAGON: Then tell him to keep his grubby palms off her!

MAITRE JACQUES: Will do. *(Goes to CLEANTE.)* Well, Monsieur Cleante?

CLEANTE: I am sincerely smitten with a sweet sausage of a girl called Mariane, and she loves *moi*. But he's gone and spoilt it by sneaking in and stealing her!

MAITRE JACQUES: Oh! He's flat out in the wrong there, sir.

CLEANTE: Marriage, at his age! He's ready for his coffin!

MAITRE JACQUES: It's the girl I feel sorry for. I'll tell it to him straight. *(Runs to HARPAGON.)* Fear not, sir, I've told him what's what. He admits to acting like a prize 'nana and agrees to respect your wishes in respect of your choice of wife as long as you respect his choice of wife in respect of it not being your choice of wife.

HARPAGON: Fine. If he accepts that Mariane is mine he can marry whoever the hell he wants!

MAITRE JACQUES: Gotcha! *(Runs to CLEANTE.)* So, I've read him the riot act and he took it like a man. Says he was only off with you for bein' off with him, so if you hold off being off with him he's on with you and her getting off and off with being off, are we on?

CLEANTE: Er, yes, I think so. If I can marry Mariane I shall be as docile as a milquetoast, as servile and submissive as a shepherded sheep!

MAITRE JACQUES: *(Wipes face.)* I'll pass that on. *(Runs to HARPAGON.)* He's caved, sir. Agrees to all your demands.

HARPAGON: Splendid!

MAITRE JACQUES: *(To CLEANTE.)* Folded like a cheap suit, sir. The girl's yours.

CLEANTE: Sensational!

MAITRE JACQUES: Now, might I suggest we end this with a gentlemanly handshake?

They shake hands.

CLEANTE: Thank you, Maitre Jacques! King Solomon himself could not have judged it more wisely.

CLEANTE gives him a bank note. HARPAGON doesn't want to lose face.

HARPAGON: Yes, thank you, Maitre Jacques, your efforts are much appreciated.

He gives him the bank note attached to a string. MAITRE JACQUES pockets both notes.

MAITRE JACQUES: Thank you.

MAITRE JACQUES moves to exit. Just before the string becomes taut he produces a pair of scissors and snips it...

CLEANTE: Oh, Pa-pa, you really are the best and kindest father a son could wish for.

HARPAGON: To be a kind father is easy when one's son is so gracious and wise. Cleante, perhaps I could afford to give you just a little money to set you on your way as a married man.

CLEANTE: That's very kind, Pa-pa, but now you've given me Mariane I have all I need.

HARPAGON: Indeed, but you… Say again.

CLEANTE: Now that you've given me Mariane I have all I could wish for.

HARPAGON: Sorry, run that past me one more time.

CLEANTE: Now that you've given me Mariane –

HARPAGON: Who said anything about giving you Mariane?

CLEANTE: Why, you did, to Maitre Jacques.

HARPAGON: No, you told him you'd give her up.

CLEANTE: *Au con-bloody-traire!* I said I should never give her up. And now I am more intent than ever to marry her!

HARPAGON: As am I!

CLEANTE: Well, it's me she loves! She thinks you're a cheese-paring miser with a face like a shaggy ram's flank!

HARPAGON: Well, at least I'm not some bed-wetting pimple-chinned coxcomb with the voice of a thimpering thchoolgirl! You are no longer my son!

CLEANTE: Best news I've had in years!

HARPAGON: And don't imagine you're getting a penny of my money. I disinherit you! And Elise gets nothing either because she's a girl, so even after I die I'll be richer than both of you!

CLEANTE: If that means we're free of you I should call that a bargain!

HARPAGON: A bargain he calls it with his famous head for business! Just what kind of bargain is it, tell me, when I have all – the girl, the money – and you have nothing? Eh? Kiss! My! Breeches! I don't know why I ever bothered having a family in the first place! I should have just stuck with my money – it gives me everything a family might, and more. Money doesn't answer back! Money doesn't dress itself up in velvet and lace like some flippety flappy flowery flipping fopdoodle. You make me look a fool! And money doesn't try to stab me in the back either! From now on, it's just me, my wife and my money! Which no one, my son, will ever find!

Exit HARPAGON. LA FLECHE holds up a strongbox.

LA FLECHE: I've found his money, sir, follow me! Come on! Better to be born lucky than rich, they say, and we're in luck!

CLEANTE: I'm sorry, I really don't follow…

LA FLECHE: Maitre Jacques told me all about it, and Frosine told me her plan to solve it. All that blinkin' palaver with dressing up as a Viscountess!

CLEANTE: You understood her plan?!

LA FLECHE: Yeah, and it involves too much acting for my liking. This'll be loads quicker. We can make 'im do anything if we hold his money to ransom!

HARPAGON: *(Off.)* Oh my darlings…

LA FLECHE: That's him coming now, quick run!

Exit CLEANTE with LA FLECHE. Enter HARPAGON who starts to look through his tomato plants.

HARPAGON: Have you missed me? What's this? My hiding place discovered? My money dug up? Stop thief! Somebody stop the thief! Justice! Give me justice! Everything is lost! My money! My precious money! Where is the thief? Where? There! There? Left? Right? There! Where? Aha! Got you!

He has tangled himself in his cloak.

HARPAGON: Yes, I know what I'm going to do with you, my lad! Ha! Aggghhh! It's me! I've caught myself! I'm going mad! What's happening here? What am I doing? Where am I? What am I? Who am I? My lovely money, my sweet darling money! My honey money. They have taken you from me. Torn asunder! Cruelly ripped from my breast. Without you I am nothing.

HARPAGON leans against the drainpipe of the greenhouse, which gives way, and he is drenched in rainwater

HARPAGON: You are my one and only. My joy, my light, my beautiful, consoling, lodestar of loveliness. Lantern of truth. Without you, life isn't worth the living. What is a person without their money?! Nothing! I'm finished. I'm dying. I'm dead. I'm buried. Mourners sing psalms at me, the priest throws dirt in my grave, and the passing parade moves on. Alas, poor Harpagon – and I mean poor! Will no one lift a finger to help him? Resurrect me? Lift me from this Hades of moneylessness! I beg you – tell me who it was… You! Whisper it to me! What do you mean you hate audience participation? You're a witness! Or an accomplice! Yes!! You all are! This was obviously an inside job! I'm going to take this all the way to the High court. I'll have everyone here tortured for information! Even you lot! To hell with your statutory rights! We can waterboard you these days if we want to. You all came to laugh at me, didn't you?! Well you'll be laughing on the others side of your ugly faces by the time I'm finished with you! I can tell the guilty ones, you know! You… you… definitely you! You up there, restricted view, don't think you're immune! It's a huge conspiracy!! You know who did it, but you're not saying are you?! Ushers, lock the doors, no one's leaving!

HARPAGON staggers around, clutching his chest…

HARPAGON: Arrggghh! Oh my God, I'm going to have a heart attack! Is there a doctor in the house? Yes? Well piss off and get a policeman! Somebody build a gallows – I'm going to hang you one by one 'til somebody owns up! And if no one owns up, I'll hang myself!

An OFFICER of the law enters.

OFFICER: Hello, hello, hello?

HARPAGON: Hello!

OFFICER: Hello?

HARPAGON: Ah, hello… who are you?

OFFICER: An Officer of the Law.

HARPAGON nods to the audience.

HARPAGON: Good work, Doctor! Come this way, Officer!

ACT FIVE

Inside the house. It is decked out for the wedding party. DAME CLAUDE is finishing putting up a line of old bunting that reads: 'Welcome M. Harpagon and your bride Beatrice'.

HARPAGON: *(To DAME CLAUDE.)* Change that to Mariane will you?

OFFICER: Leave this to me, sir. This is not the first burglary I've been called to – far from it. If I had a gold coin for every man I've had hanged, I'd have one gold coin. Now, how much did you say was in this chest?

HARPAGON: Ten thousand. Cash.

OFFICER: Quite a bit then, a serious crime?

HARPAGON: Yes, a serious crime! I tell you, hanging's too good for the kind of rogue that would do this to a man. Find the culprit and torture him.

OFFICER: Torture?

HARPAGON: Torture him! Chop his thieving fingers off and serve them to him in an omelette! Without a side salad!

OFFICER: And is there anyone you suspect of perpetrating the theft? Anyone been sniffing about, that kind of caper?

HARPAGON: Everyone! Arrest everyone! Everyone here and everyone out there and torture them all until we have our thief! And if that doesn't work then torture yourself!

OFFICER: I appreciate your desire to bring this matter to a head, sir. But experience tells me we shall be best served by a more careful approach. Slow and steady wins the race.

MAITRE JACQUES enters at speed, calling offstage.

MAITRE JACQUES: Don't let him go! Slit his throat! Grill his feet! Plunge him into boiling water then hang him from the ceiling!

HARPAGON: Who, the thief?

MAITRE JACQUES: No, the suckling pig we're having for dinner. I'm really going to town on this one!

HARPAGON: Maitre Jacques, this gentleman would like to ask you a few questions.

MAITRE JACQUES: Go ahead, but I never reveal my culinary secrets!

HARPAGON: Not about the food, about my money, you juggins! It's gone!

MAITRE JACQUES: Lost some money, have you, sir?

HARPAGON: No, I didn't lose it! It's been snitched! *(Grabs MAITRE JACQUES by lapels.)* And someone is going to pay!

OFFICER: All right, sir, go easy. There's a way of dealing with people like this. He seems decent enough. No need for prison for his sort…

HARPAGON lets MAITRE JACQUES go. OFFICER suddenly grabs MAITRE JACQUES, slams his head on the harpsichord and holds his arm behind his back.

OFFICER: Because he's going to confess now! That's it, my lad, spill the beans, and I'm not talking *haricots verts*! You might even get a little reward from your ever-loving master here!

HARPAGON: He won't, but carry on.

OFFICER: Go on. Sing like a tweety bird.

MAITRE JACQUES: *(Aside.)* Here's my chance! I knew it would come! I'll get my own back on Valere and ruin him in the eyes of my master! What that man did to my baguette…!

HARPAGON: *(Twists ear.)* Is this an aside? If so, it's going on far too long.

OFFICER: Steady, sir. You have no authority to administer physical punishment. I, on the other hand…

OFFICER slams sash window down on MAITRE JACQUES' hands.

MAITRE JACQUES: All right, all right, I'll tell you who done it! Just let me go and I'll tell you!

OFFICER lets go.

OFFICER: Tweet tweet.

MAITRE JACQUES: The thief that you seek is indeed of your own household, Monsieur Harpagon, sir. It is none other than your butler, Valere!

HARPAGON: Valere?

MAITRE JACQUES: Valere!

OFFICER: Valere.

MAITRE JACQUES: Valere!

DAME CLAUDE: Valere!

MAITRE JACQUES: Valere!

HARPAGON: Valere?!

MAITRE JACQUES: Valere, yes, Valere! Are you deaf as well as tight? I'm certain of it.

HARPAGON: Why?

MAITRE JACQUES: Well, stands to reason.

HARPAGON: Whose?

MAITRE JACQUES: Mine!

OFFICER: We shall need a little more to go on. Evidence. Details.

HARPAGON: Did you see him lurking where I'd hidden my money?

MAITRE JACQUES: That's right. Where was it again?

HARPAGON: In the greenhouse, under the tomatoes.

MAITRE JACQUES: Exactly! I saw him lurking in the greenhouse under the tomato plants, holding… What was your money in?

HARPAGON: A strongbox.

MAITRE JACQUES: As I thought! I saw him lurking in the greenhouse with a strongbox!

OFFICER: Describe it.

MAITRE JACQUES: It's about twelve foot by twelve, low brick wall, with panes of glass.

HARPAGON: Not the greenhouse, the strongbox, fool!

MAITRE JACQUES: Oh, er, well, it was… big?

HARPAGON: Mine was small.

MAITRE JACQUES: That's what I mean, it was big for a small strongbox. Or small for a big one, 'pends how you look at it. The contents were certainly big.

HARPAGON: What colour was it?

MAITRE JACQUES: Colour?

OFFICER: You heard him!

MAITRE JACQUES: Magenta! No, that's ridiculous. Was it a warm colour? Starting with the letter…

HARPAGON: It was grey.

MAITRE JACQUES: G! For grey! A small grey strongbox in the greenhouse under the red tomatoes! With the lead piping!

HARPAGON: It's mine all right! Clear as day! An open and shut case! Take his statement.

OFFICER: Very good, sir.

HARPAGON: Oh, why did I ever trust that Valere?

Enter VALERE.

VALERE: Ah, sir, there you are! I wish to speak with you about your daughter.

MAITRE JACQUES: Here's the disgraced charlatan himself, sir.

HARPAGON: Valere, come here, stand before us. And now admit to the most vile and contemptible crime ever committed.

VALERE: Is everything all right, sir?

HARPAGON: 'Is everything all right?' he says! Feel you no shame for your misdemeanours?

VALERE: I'm confused, what misdemeanours are they?

HARPAGON: Oh, don't play the innocent with me, viper! You know damn well! To think that you would take advantage of my generous nature! Insinuate your way into my house, my trust! Tis villainy, say I, villainy on a massive and repugnant scale!

VALERE: Then since it seems you know everything, sir, I shan't attempt to deny it.

MAITRE JACQUES: *(Aside.) Sacre Blimey!* Seems I stumbled on the truth without even knowing it!

VALERE: I've been meaning to speak up, I just couldn't find the right moment. But since it's all out in the open, I can only hope you'll give me a fair hearing.

HARPAGON: Oh, I'll give you a fair hearing all right! Followed by a fair hanging, you traitorous pigshit!

VALERE: There is no need for such insults. I see I have offended you, but my offence is surely forgivable.

HARPAGON: Forgivable?! A cold-blooded stab in the back and he calls it forgivable! *Et tu, Brute*, right in the kidneys! 'Forgivable' says the man who drains me of my blood!

VALERE: In the matter of your blood, sir, mine shall not disgrace you. Your honour will not be tarnished.

HARPAGON: To hell with honour! What made you do it, that's what I want to know?

VALERE: I can only blame that most powerful of gods that is the god of love, sir. Material considerations played no part. I only ask you let me keep what treasure I already have. You would not lose that treasure just by allowing me to have it –

HARPAGON: The man speaks gibberish! Love of money's sent him soft in the head!

VALERE: ...for I am tied to what is your own forever. Only death can unbind us.

HARPAGON: Then death it must be!

VALERE: Oh dear.

HARPAGON: We'll do it here. Where's my hangman?

MAITRE JACQUES: That would be me, sir!

HARPAGON: Ay, you, fashion a noose, he's confessed. Officer, tie his hands.

OFFICER: Er, yes, very good, sir.

MAITRE JACQUES throws a rope over a beam in the ceiling...

VALERE: Do as you will but allow me one last request: that you lay the blame at my door and no one else's. Do not punish your daughter.

HARPAGON: Punish Elise? Why would I punish Elise?

VALERE: Thank you, sir! In saying these words you do me a great kindness.

HARPAGON: Now do me a great kindness and show me where you've hidden my treasure!

VALERE: I have not hidden your treasure, sir. She's here within the house as ever.

HARPAGON: Then fetch it! *(Aside.)* What a loon! He thinks my treasure a lady! *(To OFFICER.)* Officer, go with him. Don't let him escape!

VALERE moves to leave, accompanied by OFFICER.

HARPAGON: Ah-ah, wait a minute! You haven't tampered with it, have you?

VALERE: Tampered?! Why, no sir, most assuredly not!

HARPAGON: Shoved your grubby mitts in and grabbed a handful?

VALERE: No sir!

HARPAGON: Licked at the gravy, had a nibble on the crackling?

VALERE: No sir, no, and most categorically no! With such accusations you wrong us both! I should rather die than offend her modesty!

HARPAGON: *(Aside.)* He sounds more like an Italian soprano serenading his lover!

VALERE: Maitre Jacques knows the truth. *(Aside to MAITRE JACQUES.)* Please, Maitre Jacques, I know I have offended you, but for love's sake tell him what you know.

MAITRE JACQUES: Oh all right! 'Tis true, sir, I have witnessed them courting. And he did seem to show full respect to her lady's modesty. But can we hang him anyway?

HARPAGON: Modesty? Courting? What are you talking about?

VALERE: Why, your daughter Elise of course. It wasn't until this morning that she finally gave me all I desire by consenting to marry me.

HARPAGON: My daughter has promised to marry you?

VALERE: Ay, sir.

HARPAGON: Then this is a double catastrophe, a multiple felony! *(To OFFICER.)* Come, Officer, do what you must. Draw up the paperwork. Hangman, this rogue must be hanged for theft and unauthorised interclass household seduction!

VALERE: But sir, this is a travesty! If you would just let me tell you who I am…!

Enter ELISE, with a cheap stuffed toy and a toffee apple.

ELISE: We had such larks, Pa-pa, the coconut shy was *tres amusant*, and I bumped into a rich widow who … Valere?!

VALERE: Elise, my darling, I'm afraid my war is over. I have been subjected to summary court martial and it has been decided that I shall be demobbed from this mortal coil.

ELISE: Noooooo!

HARPAGON: You see now where your silliness gets you, daft, unworthy and susceptible daughter. You really don't deserve a father like me.

ELISE: I quite agree!

HARPAGON: And we'll have less of your cheek! Is this what your expensive upbringing has taught you? To fall for a wretched thief, to engage yourself to a cheating ne'er-do-well? Repent, both of you! You in a convent and you at the end of a rope!

VALERE: No. We will not let the hysterical ramblings of one man condemn us. I demand to be heard properly before I am judged.

HARPAGON: All right, no hanging. We'll burn you at the stake!

ELISE: Father, these accusations are rashly made! Please, show mercy! Refrain from rage; refrain from rendering your parental rights so randomly and unrestrainedly; refrain from ridicule and wrongful arrest! Valere is not what you think. Without him I would be dead, metaphorically and literally.

MAITRE JACQUES lights a match which is instantly blown out by VALERE.

ELISE: Yes, dear father, he is the heroic man who saved me from drowning.

HARPAGON: Oh, for the last time! You were in a pedalo in the lake at the Bois de Boulogne!

ELISE: Yes, father! That is where he so courageously saved my life!

HARPAGON: The water was knee-deep!

ELISE: Father, I beg of you...

She grabs his leg, he walks across the room, dragging her behind him...

HARPAGON: No, the law must be seen to be done. Valere must be made an example of.

MAITRE JACQUES douses petrol on the bushels and strikes a match.

HARPAGON: He will be hung from the neck until he be dead!

MAITRE JACQUES frustratedly blows out the match and readies the makeshift noose.

VALERE: Must I submit to the rough justice of war?!

HARPAGON: Yes!

The doorbell rings. MAITRE JACQUES puts on his footman garb, and answers it. Enter MONSIEUR ANSELME.

MAITRE JACQUES: Monsieur Harpagon, sir. Our neighbour Monsieur Anselme has arrived!

ANSELME: Whatever is the matter, Monsieur Harpagon? You look so very upset!

HARPAGON: Upset?! I'll say I'm bloody upset!

VALERE: You're upset? I'm about to be hanged!

ELISE: You're upset?! With you dead, I'll have to marry him!

HARPAGON: Monsieur Anselme, you see before you a most unfortunate man. Me. This double-crossing rogue has inveigled his way into my house, become my butler by bogus means, seduced my daughter and stolen my money!

VALERE: *(To MAITRE JACQUES.)* Why does he talk of money all the time?

ELISE: He never seduced me, I loved him from the start! And we never went all the way, we drew the line at heavy petting.

HARPAGON: What's more, they have signed what I believe will become known in future centuries as a pre-nuptial agreement, so you are insulted too.

ANSELME: But sir, I have no desire to marry Elise if she does not wish it. Nor claim a bride whose heart is promised elsewhere.

HARPAGON: Then you're a better man than me. Officer, charge this miscreant for his crime and do it quickly.

VALERE: Since when is love a crime? Is love of money not a greater crime than my crime?

ELISE: And Pa-pa! Wait 'til you find out who he really is!

HARPAGON: So you keep saying. Forgive me if I don't leap with joy at yet another cock-and-bull story of noble breeding. You can't move these days for lying peasants claiming they're the 7th Count of this or the 9th Duchess of that! Hang him...!

ALL: Hooray!

Enter CLEANTE in a manufactured state of wild excitement. ALL despair at another delay to the hanging.

85

CLEANTE: Bless my soul and blow me tight – I have the most remarkable news! *(Aside, to ELISE.)* I understand the plan! *(End of aside.)* A most esteemed guest is newly arrived and most insistent upon meeting you, Pa-pa! She is none other than that most renowned beauty, Viscountess Frangiapane Choufleur! 9th Countess of Pate De Foie-Gras! 27th Marquesse of Moules Marinières! Accompanied by her loyal maid Frou-Frou!

Enter FROSINE in elaborate costume with garish make-up, crazy wig, etc. She is accompanied by MARIANE, who plays Frou-Frou, her lady-in-waiting.

ELISE: Bless my sainted pettipants! Pa-pa, 'tis the rich widow I met at the fair!

FROSINE: *(As VISCOUNTESS.)* Forgive, please, this unheralded interruption. I was passing through Paris and heard that the famous Monsieur Harpagon was quite the most handsome man in France.

MARIANE: *(Terrible hammy acting.)* Indeed, Madame, he is a most impressive figure of a man, like a falling star heaven-sent, or a ripe, unblemished fruit upon a silver bough. And yet I blush, for I fear he may be able to hear me speak of him.

FROSINE: Blush not, for there is no shame in identifying true beauty. So taken am I, indeed, by his good looks and charm that I can quite imagine taking him for a husband and placing my considerable assets in his hands. *(Offers hand.) Enchanté*, Monsieur Harpagon.

HARPAGON: Sod off, Frosine. And as for you, my future wife, I would have expected better.

MARIANE: Better acting or behaviour?

HARPAGON: Both! *(To VALERE.)* That was your idea, was it? To distract me with a fake *grand dame* while you made off with more of my belongings.

CLEANTE: *(To ELISE.)* Is the plan working?

VALERE: No, sir, I would never falsely claim a title for myself or anyone else. Nor, in my case, would I need to since all of Naples can testify to my birth and family.

ANSELME: Careful, young man. I know Naples very well and shall soon know if you're lying.

ELISE: He's not! He's not!

VALERE: If you know Naples then you will recognise the name of Don Thomas D'Alburcy.

ANSELME: Indeed. I think it safe to say that no one knows that name better than I.

VALERE: Well, that man was my father.

ANSELME: Young man, you don't expect us to believe that you are the son of Don Thomas D'Alburcy?

VALERE: Ay, sir!

ANSELME: Well, damn your impudence! Using a deceased nobleman in your attempt to deceive us! I must tell you that the man of whom you speak is widely understood to have been lost to the sea some sixteen years ago, along with his wife, daughter and son.

VALERE: And I must tell you, sir, that you are wrong! For Don Thomas' son was saved from that wreck by a passing Spanish vessel, as was one of his servants. And it is that son who addresses you now. For the Spanish sea captain was a kindly man who took pity on me and brought me up as his own until, on reaching adulthood, I became a soldier. Whereupon I learned that my father was not dead but now living hereabouts! So I came in search of him, and that was how, in another shipwreck, I came to meet my dear Elise. Well, such was my love for her, and such was her father's intransigence, I resolved to become a servant in his house, and here I am.

ELISE: It's true!

ANSELME: For all we know this could simply be a well-told story of your own invention. What proof do you have?

VALERE: I have several. I have the Spanish captain who will vouch for me. I have this ruby signet ring which belonged to my father. And old Pedro, the servant who was rescued with me, who has stayed by my side ever since. Pedro!

Enter PEDRO in Spanish national costume.

PEDRO: Iss true! Eee izz dee thun of Don Thomath d'Alburthy!

VALERE: *(Reveals necklace.)* I also have this: a necklace given to me by my mother, from which hangs but a fragment of a sovereign, the other part of which I believe…

MARIANE: …was hung around your sister's neck, just hours before you were separated…! *(Reveals necklace.)* Valere, I am that sister!

They bring the pieces of the sovereign together.

ANSELME: Heavens, what fortune! Is it a match?

VALERE: It is, it is!

MARIANE: It is, it is!

MAITRE JACQUES: *Crème brûlée!!*

ELISE: It's all too much!

ELISE faints.

MARIANE: I knew it the moment you opened your mouth to speak. And as you did so the final pieces of our family's story fell in place – a story that our mother has told me oh so many times. I could weep for happiness, and she will too! For we too survived that shipwreck, but our rescuers were not benevolent Spaniards but black hearted English pirates. Ten long years we spent in captivity, suffering their coarse ways, their warm beer and their dreadfully under-seasoned food.

ALL: Urgh!

MARIANE: And only by luck, in another shipwreck no less, did we manage to escape. And since that time we have lived in Paris and known nothing but hardship.

ELISE revives.

ANSELME: And yet you survived, and so did your brother. A divine miracle if ever there was one! Now, come to me both, embrace me both, for I am your father!

ALL: Nooooooo…!

MAITRE JACQUES: This is too good. I should write it down and sell it as some sort of theatre play!

VALERE: You, sir, my father?!

ANSELME: Quite so.

ELISE: Daddy, you were going to make me marry the father of the man I love!

HARPAGON: Yes, but free of charge!

MARIANE: It's you, sir, that my mother weeps for every day?!

ANSELME: 'Tis I, Don Thomas D'Alburcy, saved from the depths all those years ago with my riches safe and sound. After sixteen years of believing you dead, wandering this Earth in a fog of grief, my thoughts did finally turn to finding a companion, a good and sweet-natured woman that might finally heal my wounds. And so I settled here in Paris, calling myself Anselme, hoping to forget the sorrows I associate with my former name.

HARPAGON: So this reprobate's your son, this is what you're telling us.

ANSELME: Ay, sir.

HARPAGON: Very well, then it is you I shall sue for the ten thousand crowns he stole from me.

VALERE: I never stole ten thousand crowns. Who told you that?

HARPAGON: *(Points to MAITRE JACQUES.)* He did!

MAITRE JACQUES: I don't recall saying that, no, not exactly…

HARPAGON: You can't go back on it now, the officer wrote it down!

OFFICER: It's true, I have it here. Read it and weep!

VALERE: But you don't really think me capable of such a thing?

HARPAGON: What I think is immaterial. All I know is I want my money!

CLEANTE: And you shall have it, Pa-pa! But first you must stop this lunacy! I know where your money is, and I shall get it back to you if you consent to my marriage to Mariane.

ELISE: Cleante, what are you talking about?

CLEANTE: I had a back-up plan! You see, my ex-valet...

HARPAGON: Shut up and tell me where it is.

CLEANTE: It's somewhere very safe. Now make your choice, Mariane or the money.

HARPAGON: And it's all still there, you say?

CLEANTE: Not a sou has been lost. Mariane's mother has sent word: as a loving parent she will let her daughter choose between us. Will you do the same?

MARIANE: Cleante, my mother's word is one thing, but surely my long lost brother and father must have their say. You must ask my father for my hand.

CLEANTE: But of course. Monsieur Anselme –

ANSELME: Young man. Fate hasn't brought us all back together so that I can deprive my daughter of happiness. Monsieur Harpagon, please accept that any young lady would prefer the son to the father and join me in blessing this double wedding.

HARPAGON: All right. As long as my money's safe.

CLEANTE: It is, I promise you!

HARPAGON: And I'm not required to pay any dowries, sinecures, salaries or inheritance.

ANSELME: I shall cover all expenses.

HARPAGON: For their *(ELISE and VALERE)* wedding too, not just theirs *(MARIANE and CLEANTE)*?

ANSELME: Of course.

HARPAGON: And you'll pay Madame Frosine's matchmaking fee?

ANSELME: I'll double it!

FROSINE: I told you I was good!

HARPAGON: And you'll buy me two new suits, one for each occasion?

ANSELME: It would be my pleasure.

HARPAGON: Then we are all agreed. I think I've been very generous, don't you?

ALL: Oh yes, yes, absolutely!

HARPAGON: Right. Good. Where's my money then?

CLEANTE: It's in your safe place, behind the painting, silly!

He takes the strongbox from the safe place.

ANSELME: This calls for a celebration.

A party begins. CLEANTE gives HARPAGON the strongbox.

CLEANTE: Your strongbox, father, all present and correct.

HARPAGON: Oh, my money, my money!

ELISE: Father has re-found his truest love!

OFFICER: Here, hang about. What about my money? Who's going to pay for these legal documents? I've already drawn them up.

HARPAGON: Take Maitre Jacques. You can hang him for perverting the course of justice. And for crimes against music!

MAITRE JACQUES: Typical! I tell the truth and get beaten up. I tell a lie and get the death penalty. This whole tale is the epitome of mordant wit!

ANSELME: Officer, I'm sure we can forgive this servant his little deception.

VALERE: Little? It could have been me for the gallows!

ELISE: But now it's you for me for the rest of our natural lives.

ANSELME: Now let us send for your mother, children, that she may share in our happy news.

FROSINE: No need, sir, for I am here. For after that ship went down... Just kidding!

ANSELME: Come, mischievous lady of the night, let us all share our happiness together! Music!

MAITRE JACQUES plays the harpsichord. They begin a joyous dance.

HARPAGON: Well said, Monsieur! For today's events have taught me there is no happiness in this life that does not come from the true love of one's family!

FINALE

ALL: *(Except LOVERS.)*
They're in love!

LOVERS:
We're in love!

HARPAGON:
But love costs money
Costs money
Costs a lot of money
Costs money
Are you sure?

LOVERS:
We're in love!

HARPAGON
Damn!

LOVERS:
Very much
Very much in love

ALL:
For love prevails and cupid's bow
Is twanged a-fresh to bathe our show
In a rosy pink champagne-ish glow
Of love's sweet holiday

MAITRE JACQUES:
God help us!

ALL:
Death's sojourn is placed on hold
For love's a flame will ne'er grow cold

And sure as sunshine smiles above
We'll be saved
For ever and a day
By all-redemptive love
We'll be saved
For ever and a day
By lovely, lovely love

MAITRE JACQUES: Dance break!

They all dance.

GIRLS:
Lovely love is lovely lovely

BOYS
Loveliest of all is lovely love

MAITRE JACQUES: I'm gonna be sick!

GIRLS:
Love is really lovely but the loveliest of loveliness is love

ALL:
Lovely lovely love

MAITRE JACQUES: I have been sick!

ALL:
We'll be saved forever and a day by

GIRLS:
Lovely lovely lovely lovely

BOYS:
Lovely lovely lovely lovely

ALL:
Lovely lovely lovely lovely love

HARPAGON:
And money!

(END.)